What people are

The Philosophical ~~Conversation~~

The lightest practical and most theoretical introduction to philosophical practice there is.
Extract from the jury report for the Dutch version of the book, elected as winning book of the Berrie Heesen prize of the Centre of P4C in the Netherlands, 2021

It would be an understatement to describe this book as a fun read. Kristof has demonstrated how dialogue can be philosophical and practical at the same time, something unique to many Asian readers but should really be universal.
Shiro Ando, International Peace Worker (Myanmar), Author and Founder of Philosophy Squats

Following Socrates, the third Earl of Shaftesbury introduced philosophic conversations to educate the new class of citizens that emerged during the English Enlightenment; fun, humor, and art were essential for effective dialogues then as they are now. In that delightful study of the basics of philosophic conversation and for the benefit of us all, both experienced and aspiring philosophers, Van Rossem masterfully teaches us how to successfully lead enjoyable, and therefore, efficacious, conversations on philosophic topics.
Lydia Amir, Department of Philosophy, Tufts University, USA; Founding Editor of Lexington Series in Philosophical Practice; President of the Israeli Association for Philosophical Practice and Adjunct-Director of the American Philosophical Practitioners Association

A highly recommended book. Kristof's passion, dedication and valuable experience in his work can be seen in this highly schematic, fresh, clear and example-filled book. I recommend it with pleasure.

David Sumiacher D'Angelo, General Director of CECAPFI and President of CECAPFI International (Mexico City)

Fun and joy-filled, Kristof uses wonderful analogies and metaphors to bring the art of facilitating philosophical conversations to life, and deftly uses conversations in the book to illustrate the science of questioning and thinking philosophically.

Emma Swinn, MBE, President of SOPHIA Network of P4C (Europe) and Co-CEO of The Philosophy Foundation (UK)

The book offers something so rare as an enjoyable reading combined with profound lessons about how to perform philosophical dialogues professionally as well as in your everyday life. This will certainly be a book that I will use in training of teachers, nurses, social workers, leaders, to get proficient in guiding philosophical dialogues.

Dr. Ann S. Pihlgren, Research Director at Ignite Research Institute, Sweden and Spain

It is the book that every philosophical discussion leader (especially in the making) should have on his bedside table.

Peter Schmitz, Socratic moderator and philosophical practitioner, the Netherlands

A good philosophical conversation is not so easy to conduct. A good, competent, effective discussion leader (philosophy teacher) is indispensable. Grips are essential and good exercises are definitely necessary. Thanks to Kristof Van Rossem's new book, there is now a wealth of tools and good exercises. Definitely recommended for philosophy teachers and their trainers.

Dr. Natascha Kienstra, assistant professor of practical philosophy and didactics, School of Catholic Theology, Tilburg University, the Netherlands

Do you really want to learn how to conduct or guide a philosophical conversation? Then this book is a must-read. In contrast to the somewhat popular reading about Socratic conversations, this book does take the reader seriously. It is well written, nuanced and easy to understand for beginners and experts alike. Kristof Van Rossem shows that he is one of the absolute experts in the field of philosophical conversation.

Barry Mahoney, PhD student and teacher trainer, citizenship education

"Reflection begins where the expression of personal opinion is disrupted. After all, if in a conversation you only repeat what you have thought about something for a long time, you are not reflecting. One of the many wise lessons from Kristof Van Rossem's new book, in which he clearly explains the usefulness of philosophizing. And meanwhile, we will read about the inspirations and creativity of the Romanian Orchestra Lautarii. For anyone who wants to (learn to) ask compelling questions, who does not hesitate to 'question evidence' and who, in short, wants to learn how to have better conversations, read *The Philosophical Conversation*!

Jos Mevis, manager, Queresta, the Netherlands

The Philosophical Conversation

The Basics

Previous Books

Van Rossem, K. et al. (2017).
Leerling of Bekeerling? Radicalisering bespreken in de klas.
Leuven: Acco
ISBN: 978-94-6344-030-1

Van Rossem, K. (2020).
Het Filosofisch Gesprek. De basis.
Leuven: LannooCampus + Leusden: ISVW
ISBN: 978-94-014-6777-3

The Philosophical Conversation

The Basics

Kristof Van Rossem

CHANGEMAKERS
BOOKS

Winchester, UK
Washington, USA

JOHN HUNT PUBLISHING

First published by Changemakers Books, 2024
Changemakers Books is an imprint of John Hunt Publishing Ltd., No. 3 East Street,
Alresford, Hampshire SO24 9EE, UK
office@jhpbooks.com
www.johnhuntpublishing.com
www.changemakers-books.com

For distributor details and how to order please visit the 'Ordering' section on our website.

Text copyright: Kristof Van Rossem 2022

ISBN: 978 1 80341 271 9
978 1 80341 272 6 (ebook)
Library of Congress Control Number: 2022942140

A CIP catalogue record for this book is available from the British Library.

Design: Lapiz Digital Services

UK: Printed and bound by CPI Group (UK) Ltd, Croydon, CR0 4YY
Printed in North America by CPI GPS partners

We operate a distinctive and ethical publishing philosophy in
all areas of our business, from our global network of authors to
production and worldwide distribution.

Contents

Acknowledgements	1
Introduction	3
Chapter 1. The Characteristics	5
Chapter 2. The Score	16
Chapter 3. The Posture	23
Chapter 4. The Technique	38
Chapter 5. The Performance	59
Chapter 6. The Structure	90
Chapter 7. The Goal	116
Notes	129
Bibliography	133

Acknowledgements

Writing a book is a craft, just like playing music or having a philosophical conversation (I don't know about "making love" though: see the Introduction). I thank the people who helped me think up, (re)formulate, and delete sentences. As in life itself, simplifying the language has proved to be the biggest challenge.

Thanks to the editors from John Hunt Publishing—Ben Blundell, Krystina Kellingley, Tim Ward—for believing in this book. Thanks to Mollie Barker and Frank Smecker for correcting the English notes. Thank you Charles Derre from LannooCampus Leuven, Belgium, who edited the first version of the book in Dutch.

A very big thanks go to Gerald Rochelle and his wife Sarah for the corrections to the English text.

Thanks to Heleen Weber, Sandra Aerts, Sibe Doosje for their suggestions for corrections to the original Dutch text. Thanks to Sam De Vlieger for helping me correct the final version of the English text.

Thank you, Jan Bram Van Luit, for helping me with the QR codes and making the gypsy music easier to listen to.

Many of the ideas in this book came about through years of collaboration with Hans Bolten, my co-trainer of Socratic conversation leaders. I thank him warmly for so many years of inspiration and craftsmanship.

Finally, I would like to thank Viktoria Chernenko for her constant willingness to redefine concepts with me, to invent new structures, and to sharpen the score. Without her, this writing task would have been much more difficult.

Kristof

Note: Throughout the book I often use the masculine pronouns "he/him/himself." I do this only to avoid repeating awkward constructions such as "he/she" or "himself/herself." The masculine pronouns should be understood to mean "he or she."

Introduction

What do making love, playing music, and philosophizing have in common? They're all activities, but—you have to admit it—if you're doing it right, it doesn't feel like work. After all, they're all activities that bring you into "flow." They unite the will, the feeling, and the mind. They make you feel alive. The hormones in your head (oxytocin, adrenaline…) start to dance.

Making love would have been a great challenge as an analogy in this book. But music has become the main metaphor. And not Bach as a symbol of wisdom but instead a gypsy orchestra. A gypsy orchestra plays fast, in all parts, and without a score. Just listen to this fragment (you will find the link in the endnote).[1]

When you have read this book, you will be able to have a conversation in the same way that free-form music is played. As you work your way through, you will gradually become familiar with the "score" and eventually be able to interpret the melody in whatever way you choose. And like a competent musician, you will be able to play without the score.

Why on earth, you might ask, should you suddenly start having philosophical conversations instead of doing something more apparently useful, like solving the climate problem? Well, the philosophical conversation *is* useful and fun at the same time. Solving the climate problem is probably only useful. Philosophizing is fun because you are constantly surprised by the different perspectives you come across. And also because you can get a lot out of it. Many obvious things that we feel obliged to do can be questioned: that you have to look after the children, that the grass has to be cut, that you have to write a book. None of these are evidently true, perhaps only probably true. Wouldn't it be wonderful to explore such matters with others in complete freedom, without fear for your image or your position?

Philosophical conversations are not just fun. They're also useful. Recently, empirical studies have shown what a philosophical conversation "yields."[2] If you start philosophizing at school, you learn to think better. You perform better at school as well as in the outside world. You listen better; you speak better. You develop self-confidence and empathy. You become a better citizen — someone who takes care of himself/herself and of others. You may also become a better politician; you may no longer even need supporting parties to uphold your interests. Those interests are already in your own head. So maybe, using the "music" we're going to deal with here, you may be the right person to solve the climate problem after all.

So there is no time to lose. Let the gypsies take you away and, to start with, help you find out how to "tidy your room."

1. The Characteristics

On a beautiful summer's day, about 30 people have gathered in the garden.[3]

They are dressed in white and wear folkloric waistcoats. They play the violin, cimbalom, bass, accordion, horns. They start a cheerful "hora" in a fast tempo. It is exhilarating.

We are in Romania. The orchestra is called Orchestra Lautarii. The *lautarii* are people from the countryside who stop working at weekends and organize themselves into "tarafs," music groups led by a "primas," a primary soloist. These men, and also female singers and soloists, play traditional Romanian music at weddings and parties, usually several days and nights in a row. The custom has existed since the Middle Ages. There is dancing, singing, drinking. Occasionally, to amuse the audience, the lautarii also tell local stories. And when Uncle Boris has had too much tzuika at the party and starts a fight, they even act as mediators.

Like this "hora," a good philosophical conversation takes you into another world. The "primas" carries you along to a swinging world of thoughts and concepts that excite you and lead you beyond yourself. But don't be afraid: you'll always stay on solid ground. Like the lautarii who are grounded in their peasant traditions, you will stay rooted in a philosophical conversation. The conversation finds its roots in everyday life. You don't need thick books to start such a conversation. All you need is a question or a different opinion about a concept. Lots of everyday disagreements happen when arguments get mixed up with "clutter."

Right, about clutter and tidying up: you can't start more "down to earth" than clutter. It's literally on the floor.

1.1. Philosophizing is like tidying up

Dad: Josephine! You have to tidy up your room, because tomorrow the cleaning lady is coming and she wants an empty floor to clean.

(Dad can hear Josephine sighing and shouting "Yeeaaah" from her room upstairs...After half an hour, he goes to have a look and finds her playing on her phone in bed.)

Dad: Didn't I tell you to tidy your room?

Josephine: It *has* been tidied up, hasn't it?

Dad: Not at all! Tomorrow the cleaning lady is coming and it's late. Tidy it up quickly.

Josephine: But I've already cleaned it up!

Dad: How so?

Josephine: Look—everything was mixed up and now I've put everything nicely in piles: my clothes, my books, my letters! The cleaning lady then just has to put it in the cupboards.

Yes, yes, those teenagers! That's how they are: chilling out and gaming instead of working, acting free and easy. You could almost think you'd started reading a book on "how to deal with headstrong teenagers." But no, this is a book about philosophical conversations and so we are filled with joy because there is a difference of opinion! And that is what philosophers thrive on! And in this case, we are especially happy because the difference of opinion here is not about being, but about the everyday problem of tidying up. Rest assured. The philosophical conversation is as much about heavy topics such as freedom, equality, and democracy as it is about domestic problems. The difference is this: when you have a philosophical conversation, you learn to love these problems. Just read what happens next and how daughter seduces father into this love.

Dad: But they're on the floor; they should be in the cupboard!
Josephine (J): Why?
Dad: Otherwise the cleaning lady can't vacuum!
J: OK, but is my room more tidy if everything is in the cupboards? I don't have a cupboard for my letters and cards anyway!
Dad: Yes, of course. It has to go in the cupboards.
J: (Remains quiet.) Why? Why is the cupboard more tidy than the piles?
Dad: Don't be difficult now!
J: But it's the same problem every week, Dad. You see it differently from me. Why don't you sit down and we'll sort it out?
(Dad sits down next to her on the bed.)
J: So why does everything have to go in the cupboard to be tidy?
Dad: That's what we usually mean by "tidied up": everything nice and tidy in the cupboards, no more mess on the floor.
J: Who is "we" then?
Dad: Well, people here in our culture, here in Belgium.
J: But our cleaning lady is from Poland. Is it the same there? What does a Polish person mean by "tidy"?
Dad: I don't know; you'll have to ask her tomorrow.
J: But what do you think? What is the most likely?
Dad: I think she'd also say that everything has to go into the cupboards. They have cupboards there too, you know!
J: OK, but if I put everything in the cupboards and just close them, will my room be tidy?

Dad: No, you have to put it in piles first and then nicely in the cupboard. Don't just put everything in the cupboard; that's not tidying up.

J: But the floor will be clean and nobody will see it!

Dad: Yes, but there is still clutter in the room, and as soon as you open the cupboards you can see that.

J: OK, so it's not just that there should be no clutter on the floor as you said earlier. There should be no clutter at all in a tidy room, not even in the cupboards?

Dad: Yes, indeed.

Like it or not, that's the sort of thing that happens. We start by sitting down to it. We agree to approach it calmly. After all, we're not going to get rid of the stuff that's here to be tidied up; that's a different problem. So stay calm, no arguments, no fighting, no display of power. Participating is more important here than winning. Only when we have sat down in love can we examine the difference of opinion. This is done by arguing — by being as willing to convince the other person as we are to be convinced ourselves. "Convincing" is not understood here as beating the interlocutor, but as inviting the interlocutor to adopt a different perspective. Why, after all, should a closed cupboard full of things lying around make Josephine's room more tidy than piles on the floor?

J: OK, but what is clutter then? Is it enough that something is lying in piles to stop being clutter? If I get a pile of books and scatter them around — is that clutter now?

Dad: No, clutter is things that are not immediately useful and are just lying around.

J: What do you mean by "not immediately useful"?

Dad: Just stuff that's lying around but you don't use!

J: Like that old hat lying there in the corner: I don't use it — it was given to me. Is that junk, then?

Dad: No, you got it from Grandpa. That has value. Clutter has no value.

J: So is clutter things that are not immediately useful or that have no value? Or both? Or is it things that are just lying around, whatever they are?

(Dad thinks.)

Dad: No, I think it's stuff that is just lying around. I also call clothes "rubbish" when they're on the floor.

J: But those paperclips on my desk over there—are they lying around too?

Dad: No, they are just lying there.

J: What is the difference between just lying there and lying around? Are my clothes lying around or just lying there?

(Josephine points to her pile of clothes.)

Dad: No, it's not rubbish. It's not lying around; it's in piles.

J: But it's only when the piles are in the cupboard that it's tidy according to you, is it?

Dad: Yes, indeed! (Dad gets up and puts the stacks in the cupboard himself.) That's how difficult it is, you see?

Yes, the daughter is showing more patience here than the father! We are no longer on the level of something that needs to be done—tidying up. We have let go of action and are in contemplation. That is also what you do in a philosophical conversation. You contemplate or consider a concept, here "clutter." What can you rightly call clutter and what language about it is itself clutter? You do that by giving arguments and counter-arguments that help you to distinguish meaningful from nonsensical language. Here, too, counter-examples are presented: the concept is concretized, tested in reality. Are those paperclips rubbish? Does that mean that the hat is rubbish?

Doing so, of course, raises new problems, for what is the difference between "just lying there" and "lying around"? It becomes more and more complicated. And you learn to love that too. Admittedly, there is something pathological about it. You might even wonder if some people have been treated for it—until further notice and without result!

J: Yes, but the disagreement has not been resolved yet! I think tidying up is also when it's lying in piles. I agree that there should be no more clutter if you want it tidy. But it is apparently difficult to explain the difference between "lying around" and "just lying there."

Dad: Yes, that's right, it's harder than I thought. Now I do need to look further into my soup that is still on the stove downstairs.

J: Are you giving up now? Are you more focused on your soup than on our problem?

Dad: Yes, otherwise it will boil over. And it's fish soup—it shouldn't boil over! But I'll certainly want to talk more about our problem later.

Yes, that procrastination is not really philosophical on the father's part. After all, the love of truth is so great that you transcend your own neuroses or procrastination. When you have a philosophical conversation with someone, you are always prepared to make the most of it. In the world of fundamentals, of why we use concepts as we do, that is where you feel at home. So why procrastinate instead of carrying on with the matter at hand? Here again, Josephine turns out to be better at her job than the father, because she does something that you can recognize as the hallmark of a philosopher par excellence: asking questions.

J: I have one more question: you're happy now because my room is tidy, aren't you? But why?

Dad: Well, because the cleaning lady is coming! Didn't I say that?

J: No, but I mean, just like the cleaning lady, you think a tidy, clean room is important, right?

Dad: Yes, of course.

J: But why is that? Why is being clean and tidy so important?

Dad: You can't function properly if everything is lying around, can you?

J: There are many people who can, you know. Just look at Mum's car: it's never tidy, but that doesn't bother her. So why is it important to you?

Dad: I like order. *Ordnung muss sein!* (Laughs.)

J: Why? Why should there be order and not chaos? When does chaos become order anyway?

Dad: That's interesting. But can we discuss that next time? My fish soup is still on!

J: OK, I'll hold you to that!

And she will hold her father to it. Because the interlocutors encounter fundamental concepts here: order and chaos. Where do they come from? What is their relationship? How do they influence our way of thinking and our culture? Many books have been written about this; we won't solve it immediately in a conversation. Yet such a conversation about these fundamentals is useful. After all, once we have understood the complexity of such fundamental concepts and the different perspectives on them, we can better understand and put into perspective our own truths and those of others, for example about tidy rooms. This includes having a carefree existence. The philosophical conversation brings joy. Even if, in the meantime, the soup has boiled over.

1.2. Is it a philosophical conversation?

This conversation happens in the time it takes to make the soup. But even so, it is a full-blown philosophical conversation. There are several reasons for this. It begins with a rule imposed by the father: the room must be tidied up! But Josephine reduces the behaviour necessary to carry out the rule to a *difference in interpretation about a concept*: tidying up. What does "tidying up" mean in our language? Opinions are divided about this: is the room tidy if the things are in piles, in the cupboard, or both? As a father, you can ignore that problem and use your paternal power to insist on behavioural change. Unfortunately, this is how many children's philosophical interests are lost: "Just get on with it. And don't argue!" But here it is different. When Josephine asks her father to sit down, she does so because she knows that this problem cannot be solved by arguing. There is *emotional distance* between the two parties, so that means that they can look at the problem from different sides — in a philosophical conversation a view is not defended, but examined.

To discuss a philosophical problem or question, you need an *attitude of availability*. You need to pay attention and have time for the question or the problem. After all, a question like "What is clutter?" is not immediately solved. In a philosophical conversation, the interlocutors devote themselves to this difficulty together. No one needs to be helped or convinced. There is no rush, nor is there a specialist to whom one must listen. The interlocutors have no agenda other than to examine themselves and each other. In our example, Josephine succeeds quite well in getting her father interested in the problem. He even becomes fascinated at one point by the apparent difficulty in defining "clutter." He takes *joy in the process* and can let go of his craving for a solution. But the peace and quiet necessary for a philosophical conversation is temporary. His soup, which is boiling over, turns out to be more important after all. For Dad, the show must go on!

At some point in the conversation, Josephine asks whether the old hat in the corner of her room also belongs in the "junk" box. Or those paperclips. In an investigation into the meaning of a concept, participants in a philosophical conversation examine what something refers to *in concrete terms*, what it is all about. After all, if you can't point that out, there is a big chance that you're confused about it yourself. By giving examples, the problem becomes clearer and new problems arise: what is the difference between things that are not immediately useful and things that have no value? To find out all that, you need *intellectual curiosity*. In a philosophical conversation, you practice that. You learn to like nitpicking. You learn to love *complexity*.

As soon as Dad and Josephine sit on the bed, the conversation takes place among equal partners who want to investigate something together through *pure thinking*. And they do that by *reasoning* together. This is done by giving examples and arguments for a particular view. Josephine asks for an argument as to why everything has to be put in the cupboard in order to be able to speak of "tidiness." Dad's answer is not very convincing: "because that is how we do things here." Reasoning also involves providing counter-examples and counter-arguments. Josephine does this when she gives the example of Mum's car in connection with Dad's view that "you can't function properly if everything is lying around."

When Dad appears to have had enough and wants to go downstairs to finish making his fish soup, Josephine continues with the discussion: why is it so important that the room is tidy at all? She wants to get the most out of it. In a philosophical conversation, participants are willing and able to look at a problem in the broadest possible way. They are not only interested in solving their own problems; they are interested in everything. *All the evidence* in their own thinking or functioning, in the culture, in the world—everything is questioned. And such an attitude sometimes has "destabilizing" effects. When it comes to order or chaos, this may not be so bad, but when it comes to moral issues such as respect for every human being or the right to one's own opinion, it can be sensitive. However, this does not prevent a participant in a conversation from continuing to ask questions. In a philosophical conversation, every stone is turned over and the foundations are exposed—no more and no less.

Those questions, those endless questions! That is perhaps the best way to recognize ·the philosopher in Josephine: So what is clutter? Who is "we"? She doesn't assume she knows what Dad means, so she asks a question about it. She is *critical*. She has a fearless attitude. She pursues her point. Dad cannot escape so easily: "Are you quitting now?" That too is part of a philosophical conversation. After all, the questions are not only about what participants say and think; they are also about the way they think and how they are involved in the conversation. Philosophizing is something you do with all your heart and soul. Participants in a philosophical conversation are constantly willing to question *themselves* and their impact on the problem. As Socrates put it in his defense speech: "A life without self-examination is no life for a human being!"

Characteristics of a philosophical conversation

1. Presence of opposing views
2. Emotional distance
3. Attention, time, and availability
4. Presence of conceptualization
5. Presence of concreteness + abstraction
6. Interest in the process rather than in the result
7. Intellectual curiosity
8. Willingness and ability to question all evidence
9. Willingness and ability to question oneself
10. Research on the meaning of a concept
11. Questioning attitude
12. Ability to reason and argue
13. Interest in thinking in itself
14. Concentration on form and content of thought

When you see it all together, it is quite something, isn't it? It doesn't happen by itself. Like playing music with the lautarii, it requires training. Passion for thinking, as Josephine shows here, is not enough. She is still too impatient: she asks many questions at the same time. Her talent needs to be supplemented by skill. In the following chapters, you will read what you need to learn in the music school of philosophical conversation in order to play the game well.

2. The Score

It is 13 February 1959. In Costesti, a small town west of Bucharest, Gheorghe is born, a son for the Ene family. Mother, father, uncles are all lautarii, Romanian musicians. The boy is fortunate enough to be born into a family that performs as a "taraf" (musical group) at all the village's festivals.

When Gheorghe was 4 years old, he grabbed his brother's accordion and played a waltz by ear. He has been playing ever since. When he was 7, Toni Iordache, a friend and one of the best cimbalom players in Romania, gave him his stage name: "Ionica Minune" — Johnny the Miracle. Ionica Minune conquered the world and is currently one of the best accordionists around.

Ionica learned to play music by imitating what was happening around him. He taught himself the technique by ear. He never used a score. On a YouTube video you can see him playing a beautiful blue accordion at a Romanian wedding. And as is the custom, people put a lot of money into his accordion while he plays. But he does not let himself be distracted. In the midst of the festivities, he continues to play with concentration and virtuosity.[4]

When you see Ionica playing, it seems easy — a piece of cake. It is light and fast. But make no mistake: this is the result of daily practice. Holding and leading a good philosophical conversation, just as in music, is a combination of attitude and technique. You don't just do it. It takes practice and dedication, and then you can "perform" in any organization, with any group. But how do you learn to perform if you do not have a natural talent like Ionica and/or have no family of musicians around you? You have to learn step by step, and a score can come in handy. The list of postures and techniques below shows you what you need in order to hold and lead a good conversation. It also tells you what is important in such a philosophical conversation. In terms of *attitude*, the most important thing is to listen. You can read what that means in Chapter 3. The *technique* in a conversation is critical thinking. It is the least visible aspect. It's only indirectly that you can see whether a musician plays well or not. He does not show his full potential in every piece he plays, but you can see how skillful he is when he presses a note or plays a scale. These thinking skills can be observed indirectly in a conversation. In Chapter 4, you can read what they are. The *performance* of a conversation involves both the facilitator and the participants together. On the surface, you only see people who either remain silent, say something, or ask questions. In questioning and answering, the skills of all participants become apparent. The thinking skills become apparent in asking short, clear, targeted questions and in answering them briefly and adequately. But what does it take to ask good questions? How do you lead a conversation well? You can read about these aspects in Chapters 5 and 6. All chapters in which the score is explained end with a basic exercise. The objectives for these exercises can also be found in the score. They are the numbers for the different lines in the staff. The aspects of posture are indicated by the abbreviation Po followed by the number they correspond to in the score. The same applies to technique (T) and performance (Pe).

THE SCORE

1. Posture (Po)

1. You sit **still**. You literally sit still. You control your immediate, sometimes emotional or instinctive reactions or judgements in favor of greater thoughtfulness.
2. You have **confidence** in yourself. You are aware that your ideas are legitimate in themselves, just as are the ideas of all other participants. You allow yourself to express these ideas and allow others to do so as well.
3. You are **authentic**. You are willing to tell others what you really think about something or someone without playing a role. You are willing to do that at any time when someone asks you to.
4. You have an attitude of **not knowing**. You are aware that everything you know can possibly not be true. You are willing to re-examine all your knowledge, beliefs, and judgements.
5. You are **alert**: you see and hear everything.
6. You are **interested** in what someone has to say. A more advanced form of showing interest is that you show **awe** for what someone says and how he says it. After all, what someone says and how he says it is different from what you think or expect. And it is so at every moment. The fact that this is "always new" and never corresponds to what you had predicted or expected is a constant source of amazement.
7. You are **flexible**. You are open to questioning your own thoughts and behavior. You distinguish between the person and the thought or behavior. If someone disagrees with you, you do not see this as criticism

of that person, only of what he says. Flexibility also implies that you are prepared to be confronted with the possible incorrectness of your own views or the weakness of your own arguments. You are also prepared to confront others with this.

8. You are **decisive**. You are prepared to take a clear position at a given time without hiding behind vague or general formulations.
9. You are **persistent**. You persevere and do not give up researching.
10. You are **introspective**. You are constantly willing to consider your influence on others and events.
11. You **enjoy** yourself. You find joy in the process.

2. Technique (T)

1. You can distinguish what is essential from what is accidental.
2. You can follow and structure a train of thought.
3. You find different alternatives and hypotheses for the same problem.
4. You can distinguish between objective, subjective, and normative sentences.
5. You can distinguish between an idea, a point of view, an argument, and an example.
6. You can distinguish between general and more specific views and arguments (such as "It's never right" versus "Jan made a mistake").
7. You can adequately connect a concrete example or experience with a view, general train of thought, or theory; and vice versa.
8. You can make correct deductions from a thought.

9. You can find causes and reasons for something and attach the right consequences to it.
10. You can put (particular) matters into appropriate (more general) categories.
11. You can name the similarity and/or difference between concepts.
12. You can identify and name the presuppositions in a reasoning process.
13. You can help someone find the right descriptive concepts for something.
14. You hear whether a participant has a ready-made position or not (yet).
15. You can identify answers to the starting question.
16. You can understand another person's emotion and respond to it appropriately (cognitive empathy).
17. You can literally remember what someone says.
18. You can correctly interpret what someone says about their experience.
19. You can represent someone's reasoning correctly.
20. You can compare what someone says with what they themselves or someone else has said before.
21. You can detect (in)consistencies in what someone says and name them.
22. You can distinguish different types of questions and assess their suitability in a philosophical conversation.
23. You can relate what someone says in the conversation to an idea in (philosophical) literature so that it enables you to make a correct intervention.

3. Performance (Pe)

The facilitator leads the implementation of this technique. He does so by showing in his speech how to be concise and *to the point* and how to ask short questions (the basics). He constantly repeats this. The participants imitate this behavior or are instructed to do so. On the other hand, he steers the application of this technique by asking the right questions at the right moment, enabling the participant to make five movements.

3.1. The foundation

1. You express yourself concisely and clearly.
2. You express yourself appropriately. Your emotions and actions are adapted to the context.
3. You question the contradiction between the words and the deeds of the participant.
4. You give clear instructions.
5. You note the views and the arguments of the participants in their words where it is appropriate.
6. You ask one question at a time.
7. You ask short, open questions.
8. You use the other person's words in your question.

3.2. The five movements

Positioning

9. You (continue to) ask for the answer to the question.
10. You ask a participant to give the concept for something or someone's statement or behavior.

Arguing

11. You ask for arguments.

Concretizing/Abstracting

12. You ask what a word or a concept is about in concrete reality (question down).
13. You ask for examples of a view or a line of thought (question down).
14. You ask what happened in an example or story (question down).
15. You ask a participant to derive a point of view or an argument from an example or a concrete situation (question up).
16. You ask about the coherence of the arguments (question up).

Listening

17. You ask a participant to repeat verbatim what someone else has said.

Critically questioning

18. You ask for the coherence of the arguments and the opinions.
19. You ask a participant to compare concepts.
20. You are asking for positions and arguments to be compared and assessed.
21. You ask for alternative explanations for something.
22. You ask for counter-arguments to a statement.

3. The Posture

Take a look at this remarkable recording of Ionica Minune.[5]

He is playing at a party. He has sat down at a table to play for a group of guests. It seems quite late in the evening. Despite the late hour, the guests listen attentively to this child prodigy, for more than 20 minutes. In their eyes there is wonder, even amazement. They are in awe of so much talent and skill. They laugh and enjoy it all. The few who pull out a smartphone use it to film the performance. The guests are listening intently to Ionica. He is also listening as he is in permanent contact with his orchestra, even though he is sitting some distance away. He plays flawlessly to their rhythms and completes their sound even more beautifully. He does not stand in the way of beauty. The beauty happens. There is fascination and esteem. Look at the attitude of those present during this magical moment at this Romanian party. They are present; they are open to what is happening: no fear but trust, no desperation but energy, no control but pleasure. And they keep going; the musicians play all night long.

Do you still have your score at hand? There you will find essentially the same attitude. You will find verbs like "sit still," "trust," "not knowing." The core of this collection is a triptych. The first six can be summarized by the term "listening." It is being open to something other than yourself. If you cannot listen, you are only playing notes and not music. In addition, a philosophical conversation is also a question of trial and error, of asserting something and also daring to abandon it, of being flexible and going for it (Po7–8–9). Third, it also creates the person. You learn not to blame others but to consider your own influence on events, and you learn to let go of your craving for solutions in order to find joy in the process (Po10–11). The pleasure this process brings is what musicians and philosophers have in common.

3.1. Listen

Beethoven's fifth symphony begins with a rest sign. Only after that do you hear the "tadadadaa" sound, which everyone knows. The famous symphony begins with silence and ends in silence again. It's the same in a conversation. And it's the same in life itself. Life is an amount of sound in between two eternal silences.

In a good conversation you listen, just like a good musician. This means, first of all, that you hear what others are saying. If you have forgotten your hearing aid at the start of the conversation, apologize and postpone it. If you do hear the conversation, next it's a matter of listening to it as well. Second, you also listen to yourself: What are you saying? What words do you use and why? There are three main ways of listening.

3.1.1. Listening like a doctor

Sophie: London is a dangerous city. I went out once, and in a bar someone put a pill in my drink. I became nauseous.
Willy: (Sophie's companion. He is a philosopher and thinks: That's a wrong generalization; how short-sighted she must be. She's not experienced much.) Don't you think that it's a bit short-sighted to say that London is therefore a dangerous city?
Sophie: (Feeling unheard, defends herself.) No, I'm not the only one. My friend was there as well and she also had very bad experiences in London bars.

Is Willy listening here? Yes, but mainly to the voice in his own head. He immediately relates what Sophie says to his own views. He interprets it within his frame of reference and thinks that what she's said is a wrong generalization. He hears Sophie talking, but is busy framing what he hears, placing it within the context of his own experiences, opinions, judgements, and feelings. In Willy's case, being a philosopher, this is a judgement about Sophie's way of thinking. The judgement in his head has such power that it is almost impossible for him to ask Sophie a neutral question. What he asks is rhetorical: he wants to push her to agree with him. And of course she does not accept this.

Adopting this form of listening is very easy and tempting when someone tells you something that interests you personally. You then think: I recognize that. Or you concentrate on how you can apply this to your own situation. This includes: anticipating what the other person will say, making assumptions, summarizing, remembering key words, and so on.

This way of listening is not wrong in itself. It is solution-oriented, it is fast, and it distinguishes good specialists from bad ones. It is done by experts and is inspired by the need for solutions. The listener wants to calm down the tension created by the question, the story, the request of the interlocutor. This type of listening is selective and colored by one's own thinking. It is common in situations where action needs to be taken quickly: at the doctor's, as a researcher, as a plumber, when collecting data. It is a doctor's listening. It is a listening in function of a judgement. You check whether what the speaker says fits your standards, your judgement. You make a diagnosis. Because of the selection you make in what you hear, you run the risk of losing the other person. After all, you are concerned with your own goals, not automatically with those of the other person. For a philosophical discussion leader, this form of listening is not recommended. After all, you have no idea of your working material: the participant's words.

3.1.2. Listening like a coach

Sophie: London is a dangerous city. I went out once, and in a bar someone put a pill in my drink. I became nauseous.
Willy: Did that pill make you nauseous?
Sophie: Yes. At first I felt fine, but when I left, everything started to spin. I immediately thought: That's because of a pill!

Listening at this level is about focus. Here, you listen intently to every word and every nuance of the conversation. You feel the flow of the conversation and you are focused on what the other person is actually saying. You interpret the words in the context of the other person. You do not add your own words. And you ask as few questions as possible.

For the listener at this level, there are only a few options: you keep quiet, you repeat (literally) the other person's words now and then, or you ask for clarification. That is what Willy does here. He wants to hear more about "becoming nauseous." Body language and intonation are of course essential here. A question for clarification should sound neutral and interested. The same question would have had a totally different effect if Willy had frowned, crossed his arms, and raised his voice. Sophie would have felt morally judged. A moral judgement, however, is unacceptable for a listener at this level because he is not thinking, only listening.

You can also ask a question because you do not understand something. That is different from asking for more explanation. In the above excerpt, Willy does understand the word "nauseous." What he doesn't know is what it means to Sophie, and that's why he asks for more explanation. Suppose he doesn't speak English and doesn't know the word "nauseous." Then his question could be: "Nauseous? I don't understand. What do you mean by that?" You then ask for clarification. Beware: this is only a question that will help the coach to continue listening. What is "nauseating" does not need to be clarified for Sophie; she already knows it. So, in a way, such a request for clarification is a weak moment, because the listener is bringing attention upon himself. However, he needs it in order to continue listening.

A condition for being able to listen at this level is that, as indicated above, you do not "think" — in the sense that you have no opinion about the content of what the other person is saying. Only when your head is empty can it fill itself with what the other person is saying. Focused listening therefore also results in memorizing what the other person is literally saying. And because you have memorized the other person's words, you can also ask targeted and appropriate questions about what has been said. The purpose of these questions can be to support the other person in his or her story, as is the case here with Sophie's story. But that does not always have to be your goal. You can also use your questions to make the other person think better about what they said or to inspire them to think differently. How you can facilitate this is described in Chapter 6. Leading a philosophical conversation starts with listening at this level.

3.1.3. Listening like a midwife

Sophie: London is a dangerous city. I went out once, and in a bar someone put a pill in my drink. I became nauseous.
(Willy looks and listens attentively. He breathes quietly, sits still, and is silent.)
Sophie: I really got scared of that kind of bar in London. But I know that it can happen anywhere. I think most of all I have had my confidence shaken. Who does this kind of thing?

The third level of listening starts from an attitude of "availability" or "presence." This attitude implies a complete openness to everything that is happening, not only in the conversation but also in the environment: the energy, the aesthetics of the environment, the emotions, the details in the speaker's body language and tone. It implies an awareness of both yourself and what is happening inside of you, and being aware of the other as always, every second, being different from yourself.

The theoretical starting point here is the structural, contextual misunderstanding of the other. After all, the other person has not only grown up in a very different meaning-context than you. He also does not always express himself adequately. Therefore it can happen that he shows something in his (body) language that does not correspond to what you think he is expressing.

Imagine the following situation: Rick is an older man who is not as confident verbally as his wife Mary. Today is a memorable day, because Mary is coming home after a week in hospital, having undergone all kinds of tests on her heart. To surprise her when she comes home, Rick has tidied up the house and prepared coffee and cake. And, because he wants to surprise her with a trip to Lourdes, on the coffee table he has spread out all kinds of travel books with pictures of Lourdes. Mary comes home and the first thing she says is: "It's always the same with you: you never tidy up after you've been reading." She walks over to the coffee table, closes the books, collects them up, and puts them back in the bookcase.

How tragic and how comical is this "all too human" situation! Despite the best of intentions, you can never be sure that the other person understands you the way you want them to understand you. These meanings are very different between people of different cultures, and even more so between men and women. The idea of "untidiness" means something different for Mary than it does for Rick. Haven't we heard this before?

Lack of understanding like this is even more fundamental than simply differences in context and expression. The other person thinks, feels, and speaks differently from you at every moment, even though on the face of it he uses the same language. Understanding him is therefore not possible in the sense that the other person believes to be the case; it does not, by definition, fit in with what you might understand it to be. To understand the other would involve reducing the other to your capacity to understand. But another person does not fit into that scheme, and his meaning is therefore by definition ungraspable. An expression like "I understand that, I have experienced that too" is nonsense because nobody experiences the same thing, not in interpretation and not in facts. You can experience similar things. But this comparison does not even occur to the discerning listener. For the same reason, the expression "I can imagine that" is also nonsense. By definition, you cannot imagine what the other person is saying. You have not been there, and what you are actually saying is: "I have now put what you are saying into my conceptual framework."

What remains, then, is silence, a *disponibilité* — an availability. Through your silence, the other person is given space and time to express what they want to express. It is close to meditation, only here the attention is completely on the event itself and not just on one's own sensation.

There are different kinds of silence: expectant, awkward, oppressive, ominous. And there are various kinds of silence when listening to someone. You have probably already experienced someone who constantly says "Hmm hmm" when you speak, but who in the meantime is miles away from you in his mind. The hmm-ing in itself says nothing about his availability in the sense of what we are talking about. Nor does the hmm-ing or silence of the listener mean that he agrees with what you are saying. Many people think that "silence is consent" and they believe that if you respond with silence or "Hmm," you agree with what they are saying. They do this because they do not understand and therefore do not respect the contextual and fundamental misunderstanding of every communicating human being at that moment.

In "available" listening, the listener makes himself open to the other. This presupposes a receptive attitude, an openness to the messages that the other person conveys. This attitude stems from a familiarity with silence, and that silence is fundamental to the process. It is the silence before, between, and after the sounds of the world, including the language people use. It is the silence of "being," of the potential of all that is. It is the silence before birth: it is the space and time in which the other reveals himself to you as other. The available listener sees every word, every gesture, as a birth of something new, not as something to be understood. Whoever destroys the silence—by placing what the other says in his own thinking—is afraid of incomprehension or loneliness. The attitude of the available listener, on the other hand, is permeated by the fundamental loneliness of every human being and, on that basis, also by the esteem and respect for the otherness of every other human being.[6]

So, in a good (philosophical) conversation you have the privilege of being present at this ongoing birth—as a midwife. Socrates, whose mother, Phaenarete, was a midwife, in a famous passage in Plato's *Theaetetus* compares his work to that of a midwife. However, Socrates says that he does not help women but men, and he "supervises their souls and not their bodies." Plato chose this image well. A good midwife is not fearful: she does not give advice, she does not interrupt, she does not impose her opinion, she does not judge, she does not think her own thoughts, in order to concentrate fully on the mother. In the words of Socrates:

> I am so much like the midwife that I cannot myself give birth to wisdom, and the common reproach is true, that, though I question others, I can myself bring nothing to light because there is no wisdom in me.
> (*Theaetetus*, 150c)

So the most important thing a facilitator must learn is to stop thinking. After all, the content comes from the others. They may be pregnant with opinions, but this should not apply to the facilitator. The head must be empty; otherwise you cannot be flexible and alert. Just like the midwife, the discussion leader is always attentive to the other person. This is not a passive attitude. The midwife is ready to intervene if necessary. She puts the birthing mother at ease, not only by radiating this basic trust but also by showing that she knows her job and enjoys it. She does not sit frantically waiting for the child; instead, she is relaxed and she smiles. She is joyful. It is a beautiful moment, even if it hurts.

In a philosophical conversation you need level 2 of listening (like a coach), but available listening (like a midwife) can also be practiced.[7] It is reflected in practicing sitting still (Po1), trusting oneself and the other (Po2), and developing regard for the other (Po6). Technically, it results in cognitive empathy (T16–17–18).

3.2. Being flexible: trial and error

Of course, this available midwife attitude only makes sense if there is also a child. Equally, drawing on our musical metaphor, there must be music. Not only should we listen, but we should also play. In a philosophical conversation, you say what you think is right to say at a certain moment, even if it still remains to be seen if it's true or if it makes sense. Decisiveness and flexibility go hand in hand. Everything you are fully convinced of, and what you say with verve, can be refuted by someone else a minute later. So much so that you may lose the plot. Then you have to admit that you were wrong and change your position. That is not easy. It requires you to be able to let go of your convictions in order to continue. Like the image of the "midwife," this double movement is a Socratic legacy. It is the merging of the "protreptic" and the "elenctic" movement.

3.2.1. The protreptic movement

In this movement, Socrates encourages his interlocutors to tell him what they think of something (Greek *protrepein* means "to urge, to encourage"). He encourages them to "play the game." In the conversation with the theologian Euthyphro, for example, the topic is what it means to be "pious." Socrates is eager to know what Euthyphro has to say about it: "So [Euthyphro], in the name of heaven, tell me now about the matter you just felt sure you knew quite thoroughly" (*Euthyphro*, 5b).[8]

Our theologian begins to talk, but soon realizes that Socrates' questions are very difficult to deal with: "Now, Socrates, I simply don't know how to tell you what I think. Somehow everything that we put forward keeps moving about us in a circle, and nothing will stay where we put it" (11b).

Socrates confuses him, but does not want him to give up: "Come, lucky friend, exert yourself! What I have to say is not so hard to grasp" (12a).

A few more attempts follow to explain to Socrates what it means to be pious, but to no avail.

Socrates continues to encourage: "So tell me, peerless Euthyphro, and do not hide from me what you judge it to be."

But Euthyphro gives up: "Another time, then, Socrates, for I am in a hurry, and must be off this minute" (15e).

The protreptic movement is the constructive part of Socrates' approach. You take a stand. The attitude is one of confidence in what you have to say, decisiveness, and persistence (Po2 + 8 + 9).

3.2.2. The elenctic movement

Constructive movement alternates with destructive movement. Euthyphro is made to doubt. It becomes difficult to maintain his position in front of Socrates. He is embarrassed (Greek *elenchos*, "shame") about his supposed knowledge of piety. In another of Plato's dialogues, Meno, a slave, aptly expresses what that experience is like after being questioned by Socrates about virtue:

Socrates, even before I met you they told me that in plain truth you are a perplexed man yourself and reduce others to perplexity. At this moment I feel you are exercising magic and witchcraft upon me and positively laying me under your spell until I am just a mass of helplessness. If I may be flippant, I think that not only in outward appearance but in other respects as well you are exactly like the flat sting ray that one meets in the sea. Whenever anyone comes into contact with it, it numbs him, and that is the sort of thing that you seem to be doing to me now. My mind and my lips are literally numb, and I have nothing to reply to you. Yet I have spoken about virtue hundreds of times, held forth often on the subject in front of large audiences, and very well too, or so I thought. Now I can't even say what it is.

(*Meno*, 80a–b)

The result of the elenchus is the experience of perplexity. The interlocutor is surprised at being so ignorant. In Socrates' work, tall trees catch a lot of wind. The more certain you seem, the harder you are tackled. And theologians like Euthyphro are among those tall trees. But Socrates does not want to humiliate. The intention is positive: after the "humiliation" comes a curiosity to know how things really are. The attitude of not knowing (Po4) is not paralyzing. It is the source of constant interest and flexibility (Po6 + 7).

3.3. The formation of the person: introspection and joy

The fact that Euthyphro runs away from Socrates will probably not surprise you. How would you deal with this? Socrates wears him down to such an extent that the answer to what it means to be pious seems further away than ever; it is worse than at the start of the conversation. Wasn't the whole enterprise to find an answer to that question? Couldn't Socrates then cooperate a little?

In this ancient text, you notice what is still typical of philosophical conversations today: they are not necessarily useful—they may not be solution-oriented. The subject might be about a question such as "What is rubbish?" But the search for the answer gets longer and longer, the problem gets bigger and bigger. Meanwhile, you are being formed as a person. You become more curious, more patient, more authentic, closer to yourself. You learn to enjoy yourself. You learn to take joy in the process rather than in the product (Po3 + 10 + 11).

The emphasis on educating the person behind the thinker is also found in most contemporary forms of philosophical consultancy or "practice." Philosophical coaches or practitioners help you to find an answer to a question you have about life, such as "Should I divorce my partner?" You search for an answer to such a question in a series of one-on-one conversations with the philosophical coach or practitioner. However, if you find a good counselor, sooner or later he will also frustrate you, just like Socrates did with Euthyphro. He will not solve your problem but will make you a better thinker, so that you can deal with your problems yourself. The counselor will make you aware of your own (limited) share in, or influence on, the circumstances. He makes you more introspective. To put it in an image: the consultant is not the light in your darkness, but he moves the curtains aside so you can see more light yourself.

Exercise in cognitive empathy

Objectives and target group
This exercise can be done with participants aged 12 years and up. It is most suitable for adults.

Objectives: Po1, Po2, Po4, Po6, T16, T17, T18

Time and supplies
You can set aside 3 x 15 minutes for this exercise. You need chairs, but not tables. It can also help if you have some cards ready for inspiration to find an experience with which an emotion is connected.

Activity
You form groups of three: a narrator, an observer, and a facilitator. The exercise is then repeated three times, with the roles changing within the group. Each turn takes about 15 minutes (timed by the observer). The sequence is always the same.

1. The narrator recounts a recent experience in which something happened that caused some feelings in him. That emotion can be positive or negative. It should be an experience that he has lived through himself, not something he has heard in the media. The narrator tells the story. During the story, the facilitator does not interrupt. He only listens and remains silent. He does not ask additional questions for more information. In his attitude he shows acceptance of the story. If the narrator asks for "support" for his/her complaint or claim, for example by asking "Don't you think this is going too far?" the facilitator does not answer. The storytelling lasts a maximum of 5 minutes.

2. After the story:

The facilitator

- first repeats the story in as detailed a way as possible in the words of the narrator;
- then asks if the narrator recognizes himself in the story. If not, he tells the story again, this time with the help of the observer;
- at the end, looks for one concept that reflects what this story meant to the narrator (e.g. "relief" or "modesty"). This is not a word that summarizes what happened in the story, but a word that represents what the meaning of this story was for the narrator. The effect should be an emotional "Yes, that's it!" It may also be a few words if one word fails (e.g. "unexpectedly disappointed"). If it is not possible to find a concept after three attempts, the observer may help.

The observer

- pays attention to the time of the session: maximum 5 minutes of story, maximum 5 minutes of repetition, maximum 5 minutes of concept search and discussion afterwards;
- writes down the narrator's story as well as he can in his own words. He uses this text to correct the paraphrase that the facilitator uses immediately after the story. He first lets the facilitator "give back" the story. If the narrator does not recognize this, he can add to it;
- searches, together with the facilitator, for an appropriate concept in case the narrator has not found it after three attempts;

- at the end of the exercise, asks the narrator how he has experienced this. He or she is asked to give a rating from 1 to 10 for the level at which they felt understood by the facilitator. Finally, the observer asks the narrator to justify this rating.

Then the roles change.

4. The Technique

Typical of Romanian accordion music are the many ornaments in the form of trills in the right hand.[9]

Instead of "E," for example, the accordionist plays "E–D–E." He does this at such a speed that it is hardly noticeable. And he does it very regularly. It gives the music a cheerful and playful sound and the musician demonstrates his technical prowess. Pay attention to the different ways he plays trills here. You will see that sometimes he does it with two different fingers on the right hand: the index finger and the middle finger. At other times he uses the index finger over the ring finger to the middle finger, which then takes the place of the index finger on that note. These finger changes go unnoticed by the average spectator. But even if you don't see it and it sounds exactly the same, the fingering has to be done this way; it is a technicality!

Even though Ionica plays without a score, he knows his notes and his ornaments. He knows every tempo change, every chord, every measure. Even before he has played the first note, he understands the music. And when he starts playing, he plays it flawlessly. After all, he has practiced for at least an hour every day. It has gotten, as they say, "into his fingers." He can play it without thinking about it and even without a score. For a band leader this is even more true: he may even know the part of every musician in the orchestra by heart.

In the second part of our score here you will find the "technique." It is a set of 23 competencies. You read verbs like "to be able to distinguish," "to connect," "to remember," "to compare." The common denominator of this is, in two words, *critical thinking*. That is not something you are born with. Not everyone can do critical thinking. You have to practice it. What you read in this section is just a start. After that, it's a matter of practicing a lot so that your thinking technique improves. There is a lot to be said for regular training exercises in critical thinking, both as preparation for and as a change from philosophical conversations. In this chapter, you will find just a few explanations of the basics of critical thinking: distinguishing between facts and interpretations, taking positions, arguing, reasoning. You will also find an introductory exercise. If you want to practice further, you will find more advanced exercises and useful literature in the bibliography.

4.1. The Martian at the bar

Take a notebook or a sheet of paper and write down: "Critical thinking begins with thinking that what you hear or read may be true but also may not be true." Now you can delete that. Is it true what you have just written down? We don't know. You will have to do further research to check whether that is true; whether critical thinking starts there. In any case, it is not true just because someone who has studied philosophy says so.

Copyright Gonzalo Orquin

This annoying skeptical attitude goes beyond just reading and listening. It is also in how you look. Just look at the picture on the previous page. Don't throw away your notebook yet; write down everything you see.

Now sort what you have written down into three columns. In the first column, write what you think is a "fact," what is objective. It is in quotation marks here, because philosophers naturally disagree about what a "fact" is and whether objectivity exists. But for simplicity's sake, we understand "objective" here as that which, for now, no one makes a fuss about. So if you have written down "two homosexual men," check with your housemate or neighbor whether they agree. If they say otherwise, then what you have written down is not objective but subjective, that is, an interpretation of the facts. Everything you have written down that you call "interpretation," you write in the second column. And in the third column, write down what you think of it in a normative sense, that is, of what you approve or disapprove. For example, maybe you think it's inappropriate or maybe you think it's perfectly acceptable. In doing this you have written down a rating, positive or negative.

Objective (facts)	Subjective (interpretations)	Normative (ratings— positive or negative)

The next task is to imagine that you are from Mars. Then go as a Martian (preferably incognito, without conspicuous space clothes) to a building in your neighborhood that has a sign on it and is called a "pub." Go inside. Ask for what the Earthlings call a "stool" and sit on it. Order something at the bar. That is the large piece of furniture in the middle of the "pub." Say "A beer" to the person standing behind it; that's always an appropriate request in such a place. You'll see that strange creatures at your side are also sitting on such stools and occasionally bringing a body part to a glass of liquid in front of them. They talk to each other. Or at least, they make noises. Now listen carefully to what the regulars to your right at the bar are saying.

Mike: (On your extreme right, next to Peter.) Hello, Peter! You look so tired!
Peter: (On your right.) Yes, how could it be otherwise? That Nancy from a few streets away organized a party at her home yesterday. And I lay awake far into the night because of the loud music. Well, if you can call it music! Fortunately John, the neighbor, called the police and they stopped it. What sort of lowlife is that? That woman doesn't belong in our neighborhood at all!

Now write down in your notebook (on the sly) one sentence of each kind that your neighbor at the bar has literally said. You will mostly hear subjective and normative statements. For example, what is "far into the night" here? That is subjective. And we don't know for sure that Nancy had organized the party. Indeed, are there any facts at all?

This critical attitude is peculiar to you because you come from Mars. You do not know what they are talking about (Po4). You are hearing everything for the first time. You are an outsider. You do not get carried away by what people around you say. You only ask yourself: how do people here on Earth refer to things? What do they mean with these words? Is what they say true or is it a misleading inference? And why do they think what they think? What a strange world this appears to be: a world of parties, loud music, and lowlifes!

4.2. Peter's position and arguments

You are still sitting at the bar. You have just heard Peter, the person next to you, say: "That woman doesn't belong in our neighborhood at all." You know the neighborhood as well and you think it's a surprising statement. You decide to get involved.

You: Why doesn't she belong here, Peter?

Peter: She doesn't belong here at all! She's the kind of person who attracts other unemployed lowlifes who raise hell every weekend. You'll see, next week it'll be the same thing, and it'll only get worse. That behavior doesn't belong here—it's a quiet neighborhood. There's nobody else here who makes a noise at night!

Now's the time to stop. But congratulations, you have taken action. Your Martian outsider attitude of "maybe so, maybe not" has not led to a forced silence. You have asked a question in a neutral, Martian way. And that question has provided explanations for what Peter said. What we have here is another competency of the critical thinker. You can distinguish viewpoints from arguments. A viewpoint is *what* someone thinks about something; an argument is *why* they think that way. Sometimes the distinction is easy to make. If you're lucky, you might hear or read a signal word like "because" or "so" and then you know that an argument or a conclusion follows. But often, as here in the pub, it is not the case. Here, the "therefore" is concealed.

Does Peter have a position here? Yes, namely that this woman does not belong in the neighborhood—not "at all." And do we have an argument? More or less, but intuitively you can sense that there is something wrong with his argument.

There are at least two problems. The first is that Nancy is said to be an unemployed lowlife. We don't know that. But even if she is, is that a reason why she doesn't belong in the neighborhood? Or is it, secondly, because she doesn't do what Peter says everyone else does, which is not make any noise at night? That's a strange view to take, to say the least. If, for example, you were dealing drugs quietly at night, would you belong in the neighborhood? What does "belonging" mean? Peter makes two classic mistakes in his reasoning:

a) He is making Nancy, who as far as we know has made a lot of noise one evening, into someone who will do so again and again, and increasingly. But we don't know that at all. He makes the mistake here of leading us down a "slippery slope" — "one thing leads to another." And that is not right, because it is not the case that because she has done this once she will do it again.

b) He equates "belonging in the neighborhood" with "doing what everyone else does, namely being quiet at night." But that is not the same thing. What everyone does is not necessarily acceptable conduct. The popularity of an act does not necessarily say anything about the quality of the act or the desirability of the act. He makes the *ad populum* mistake — it is good if you do as the majority does.

To find a way of describing your sense of the wrongness of an argument such as the one above, you can turn to the well-known "debatable reasonings" found in critical thinking literature. Below is a list of the most common ones. In all likelihood, at the top of this list would be "false generalizations."[10] Suppose your friend says: "Italy is a fantastic country. We went there last year and the weather was great, the hotel was very clean, and the people were friendly." Then it seems obvious to think: We'll go there too! But that is only until you hear someone claim the opposite about Italy. After all, you cannot conclude on the basis of one experience that "Italy is a fantastic country." It is a false generalization. Peter also generalizes when he says that "no one makes a noise here at night." It's very likely that there is one person in the neighborhood who has occasionally made a noise at night, maybe even when Peter was away. So we don't know for sure. Based on his own experience, Peter is generalizing about the whole neighborhood.

Some common reasoning methods which are debatable

- *Argumentum ad hominem* — on the man instead of on the ball: "You can't say that, because you don't have any children yourself."
- Wrong generalization: "It's always the same people who make wrong generalizations."
- Incorrect cause-and-effect reasoning: "Since that book on argumentation for schools was published, there have been fewer and fewer cause-and-effect reasonings."
- *Post hoc ergo propter hoc* — after each other but not necessarily because of each other; here, two things follow each other in time but there is no certain causal connection: "Then she bought the book on the philosophical conversation and the guiding of the conversations went much better."
- Slippery slope — one thing leads to another: "If you do those philosophical exercises with those students, the others will want to do it as well and after a while the whole school will want to. We can't get that organized."
- Straw man reasoning — subtly changing the subject: "You can't lead philosophical conversations just by reading this book!" "Yes, philosophical conversations should be used cautiously in education."
- *Ad auctoritatem* — an appeal to authority rather than a substantive argument: "It is so because I say so!"
- Wrong analogy or comparison: "This book is Chinese to me. Confucius was not an easy fellow either, it's said."

- False dilemma — it's one or the other: "Do you want to buy one book or two?"
- *Argumentum ad populum* — it's true because the majority thinks so: "Everyone has seen this show. Then so can I."
- *Argumentum ad vanitatem* — the uniqueness is enough: "This book says everything about medieval castles. It is the only book on the subject that has appeared in the USA."
- *Argumentum ad antiquitatem* — it's true because it has always been so: "You are not going to change that. We have always done it that way here."

Short exercise: Which debatable form do you recognize in the following statements?

- This school is a very good school. It has been here for a hundred years.
- There are UFOs in the city. I know a lady, not just anybody. She has had a proper training as a lawyer. She saw one in the city park.
- Porn is not harmful. Scientific research has shown that watching porn does not lead to more sexual violence.
- That lady is not fit to be a mayor. Wasn't she married to a woman?
- Tax evasion is not a sin. Everyone does it.

4.3. How Peter reasons

Mike has apparently lost interest in Peter's story about Nancy. He has started talking to the bartender about something else. You, however, do not leave it at that point. You put your notebook in your inside pocket and you decide to ask Peter a few critical questions to see if any reasonableness can be found.

You: Peter, what do you think is the main reason why Nancy doesn't belong here? Is it because you think she's an unemployed lowlife or because she made a noise at night?

Peter: It's all part of the same thing. If you have a job during the day, you know you shouldn't keep the neighbors awake at night.

You: Have you told Nancy that it's supposed to be quiet at night?

Peter: (Strongly.) No, of course not. I've only seen this Nancy once, and then only very briefly, when she came out of her house. But that's irrelevant. Everyone should know that you should be quiet at night!

You: And do you think Nancy doesn't know that?

Peter: No, otherwise there wouldn't have been an all-night racket, would there?!

You: How come she doesn't know that?

Peter: Because people like her are lowlifes; they hang around all day, don't work, don't do anything. They just don't realize that good, working people live here as well.

You: What else shows that she is a lowlife according to you?

Peter: Well, the way she looks and all that. She wears these beat-up clothes. And I wouldn't be surprised if she takes drugs; she always looks tired.

You: I thought you had only seen her once before?

Peter: Yes, but that was enough.

Oh dear, that's not going to work. You haven't made Peter think. On the contrary, you've given him the opportunity to get all wound up about Nancy. But that is no bad thing. You still have the errors in his thinking in your mind from his first statements. And in the meantime you have been able to gather lots of new material. Now it is time to take the bull by the horns. But not head-on! Be focused. You decide not to take Peter's ideas about "unemployed lowlifes" too seriously. You go back to the first question you asked about the main reason he thinks she "doesn't belong here." He has not yet answered that question.

You: Peter, what do you think the chances are that the one time you saw her briefly, Nancy was wearing clothes that you thought were worn out, but that on other days she might be dressed "normally"?

Peter: Small chance! But you never know — one day she might win the lottery. (Laughs.)

You: Could it be that it will stop with this one party and that it will be quiet at night next week and the weeks after?

Peter: There's little chance of that.

You: Have you had any problems with noise before she came to live here?

Peter: No, this was the first time. But it won't be the last time. You can bank on it!

You: Peter, suppose you are right that she is an "unemployed lowlife" or just a "lowlife," but that just this once she went crazy. Perhaps for the next few nights or weekends, or maybe even during the day, she will let her friends come into her house quietly to take drugs, just like she may have done in the past. Would she belong in the neighborhood then? I come back to my question: Is the most important thing for belonging in this neighborhood that you are not an unemployed lowlife or that you keep quiet at night?

Peter: (Is silent, thinking.) Yes, that's a good one. I think the night noise is the most important thing. At the end of the day, you don't know what people do behind closed doors. That's none of my business.

You: Is it any of your business whether she works during the day or not?

Peter: No, not really, as long as she does it quietly.

This is better. It's one–nil to you. Without making it explicit, Peter has had to abandon his whole point about the good working people in the neighborhood versus the unemployed lowlifes. As long as they are quiet. But what is "quiet"?

You: OK, and suppose the majority of the neighbors here keep quiet at night but are constantly arguing inside, throwing plates, attacking each other. Would you still call this a quiet neighborhood?

Peter: No. But people are not like that here.

You: How do you know?

Peter: (Irritated.) I don't know, but I think so.

You: But you think that a quiet neighborhood should also be quiet indoors, not only on the street at night?

Peter: Yes, that's right.

Bingo. Two–nil. The criterion for belonging here has not only been simplified (being a lowlife is out); he has also nuanced it. Now it's time to come up with a surprise shot. After all, up till now it has always been about Nancy. But Peter himself lives in this neighborhood, doesn't he? Does he belong here?

You: I imagine that you have no doubts that you yourself belong here?

Peter: Yes, that's quite natural. I've lived here for 20 years.

You: Do you belong here because you've lived here for 20 years or have you lived here for 20 years because you belong here?

This question is just to check if he goes for the first or the second argument. The first seems a kind of *antiquitatem* argument: it is because of this long-term residence that he belongs there—no reference to anything else than just this duration. The second argument is a different one and at first sight more based on reason. It could be that, for example, he was born there as well, or maybe he has relatives nearby and therefore has stayed there that long. Let's hear what his choice will be.

Peter: (Thinking.) Yeah, as I said: after 20 years it's more or less evident that you belong somewhere, no?
You: Can you imagine someone like Nancy living for 20 years in a quiet neighborhood but making a noise every day and still not belonging there?
Peter: I guess that's possible but it definitely won't happen in my neighborhood. I'd kick her out!
You: So, is the reason why you belong here more to do with this 20 years of staying at the same place or more to do with keeping quiet just like the others?
Peter: (Thinking.) Because I keep quiet. How long I've lived here doesn't really matter, when I think about it.
You: And I suppose you yourself don't have loud parties at night?
Peter: No. But I must be honest. It happened once in the past, at our wedding anniversary party. But that was seven years ago. Then, it's true, there was music all night.
You: You just said that it's also part of a quiet neighborhood that it's quiet indoors. Is that true for you?

Peter: Not always, of course. In every household there are raised voices from time to time. But most of the time it's quiet, yes.

You: So could you say that neighbors like you, who keep mostly quiet indoors and keep mostly quiet outdoors as well, belong here?

Peter: (With a clap on your shoulder.) Yeah, that's well said!

You: So could we say that if Nancy makes a noise this one time and keeps quiet indoors most of the time, she belongs here then?

Peter: (Still in doubt.) I guess so!

Yes, this is hard work for a Martian in a pub on Earth. Peter's head is buzzing with fantasies. We call them "fantasies" because there are very few concrete observations in the whole conversation. All we know is that Nancy has been causing some night-time noise, although that is not 100 percent certain. Peter says he was awake because of it, but he didn't check whether in fact it was Nancy, not even when the police came.

Peter did see Nancy once. According to him, she was wearing shabby clothes and looked tired. From this he drew the conclusion that she is a lowlife and uses drugs. We call this *inductive reasoning*. He starts with an observation of the facts (which are highly questionable here) and draws a conclusion on the basis of these. He reasons from below (the observation) to above (the thinking). The other form of reasoning is *deductive reasoning*. In this case you reason from above (thought) to below (observation). Peter is reasoning like this when he says: if you have to work during the day, you know that you shouldn't make any noise at night. And since Nancy does make noise, it must be the case that she doesn't go to work during the day. So what is the structure of Peter's reasoning here?

4.4. The mice in Peter's head

Reasoning is a sequence of positions and a conclusion. We reason all day long, mostly unnoticed. If you ask the shop assistant to wrap that voucher for your sister's birthday, the following reasoning is behind it:

1. That voucher has to be wrapped up

because

2. It's a present for my sister's birthday

and

3. Presents for birthdays need to be wrapped

Aristotle in the fourth century BC called the first part of this reasoning the *conclusion*. The second part, often occurring after the signal word "because," is the *minor argument* or the *minor premise*. We also call this the "observation argument." The third part, often occurring after the signal word "and," is the *general argument* or the *major premise*. The latter, however, is often omitted in everyday speech because it is so obvious.

If you go on asking for arguments, as you did in the pub with Peter, you get those general arguments. This is interesting because they are not always correct. They are often very obvious to the narrator but not to others. For example, when a mother says to her son: "Put your coat on, it's raining outside," she is tacitly making a reasoning that contains a number of assumptions: that you will get wet if you don't put your coat on, that you have to protect yourself from the rain because otherwise you might get sick, and that she doesn't want her son to get sick. The latter is so obvious that she doesn't mention it. Which mother would want her child to get sick? But that you get sick if you don't wear a coat in the rain is simply untrue. Some people might get sick from it, others not!

Aristotle calls the basic form of logical reasoning the *syllogism*. You have probably heard of the following syllogism:

1. Socrates is mortal
because
2. Socrates is a human being
and
3. All human beings are mortal

This is an example of valid reasoning. Logic does not concern itself with truth. Whether Socrates is mortal or not, whether all human beings are truly mortal or not, is irrelevant. Logic is about validity. The reasoning above is valid because *if* all human beings are mortal and Socrates *is* a human being, then Socrates *must be* mortal too. The conclusion then necessarily follows from the premises.

Applied to the first reasoning about the voucher, you could say that *if* presents for birthdays should (always) be wrapped and the voucher is indeed a present for a birthday, then it must necessarily be wrapped as well.

This reasoning is valid. But the general argument that "birthday presents must be wrapped" is easier to refute than "all human beings are mortal." For example, someone might say that if you give money as a birthday present, then it need not be wrapped. So, wrapping presents for birthdays is nice, but it doesn't always have to be done!

What about the reasoning in Peter's head? To get to the bottom of that, you'll have to put this book aside and do a bit of work. His reasoning is not as elegantly structured as Aristotle's. But it is a very interesting puzzle to work on. To motivate you, here are some parts of Peter's main reasoning. You will find the major and minor premises and the conclusion. Can you discover any others yourself?

Peter's reasoning:

- Those who attract unemployed lowlifes are themselves unemployed lowlifes; Nancy attracts unemployed lowlifes; Nancy is herself an unemployed lowlife.
- Unemployed lowlifes are people who have noisy parties every weekend ("stirring things up" in the neighborhood); Nancy has noisy parties every weekend; Nancy is an unemployed lowlife.
- If you have to work during the day, you know intuitively that you should not keep the neighbors awake at night; Nancy doesn't know it intuitively; Nancy doesn't work during the day.
- If you know intuitively that you shouldn't keep the neighbors awake at night, then you don't do it yourself; Nancy doesn't know it intuitively; Nancy does it.
- Lowlifes are people who make a noise at night, wear shabby clothes, and use drugs; Nancy makes a noise at night, wears shabby clothes, and uses drugs; Nancy is a lowlife.
- People who use drugs look tired; Nancy looks tired; Nancy uses drugs.
- Neighborhoods where there is no noise at night are quiet neighborhoods; there is no noise at night in this neighborhood; this is a quiet neighborhood.
- People who don't make a noise at night belong in this neighborhood; I don't make a noise at night; I belong in this neighborhood.
- People who have lived here for 20 years belong here; I have lived here for 20 years; I belong here.

It is striking that the problem is not so much the validity of this reasoning. The last argument, for example, is perfectly valid.

The problem lies in the incorrectness of the general assumptions. Most of them are not based on anything. There is an even more fundamental problem: Peter does not appear to be reasoning but is simply making statements. You have to reconstruct the reasoning in your own head. For a book like this, that's easy. But in real life you can make a mistake. The connections that you think you see between major and minor premises are not necessarily what the speaker takes for granted. So you have to listen patiently and ask questions until they are revealed.

Through your questions, you did manage to improve some of Peter's reasoning. The next two arguments don't look bad. They might even be likely.

- Quiet neighborhoods are those where it is mostly quiet outside at night and mostly quiet inside; here it is mostly quiet outside at night and mostly quiet inside; this is a quiet neighborhood.
- A quiet neighborhood is a home to people who are usually quiet at night and also usually quiet indoors; I am usually quiet at night and also usually quiet indoors; I belong here.

4.5. The Peter within: we all have presuppositions (and that's another one)

You got out of the bar, you said goodbye to Peter, and, frankly, you were glad to get rid of him. Life was easier on Mars. What do those people on Earth have in their minds anyway? Don't be surprised, though: the thinking of many people is not that much better than Peter's. It is raw and functions in inconsistent ways. It is untrained and, moreover, it functions thanks to all sorts of assumptions that are often implicit and unspoken.

When such an assumption is still open for discussion, we speak of an "assumption." What you "assume" remains to be seen if it's true or not. For example, when you say, "I suppose

Grandpa will come to the birthday party too?", you are indicating that you assume he will be there, but it is also possible that he will not. If you take cash to the shop, you assume that you can pay in cash. But when you hear that it can only be done with a credit card, you say: "Too bad. I thought you could pay in cash here."

When an assumption is no longer open to discussion and is therefore literally taken for granted, we speak of a "presupposition." This is not to be confused with a *prejudice*. If you say, "The Dutch are stingy," or "Belgians are stupid," then this is an opinion about these people that is not based on facts. It is a false generalization, often a stereotype. That unemployed lowlifes are people who wear shabby clothes and use drugs was Peter's prejudice. Voltaire apparently called a prejudice an "opinion without judgement": at this point it has not yet passed the critical test of investigating its truth.

A *presupposition* is something else. We cannot function without presuppositions. If you ask your mother, "Did you just watch television?", you presuppose that she understands it as a question and will answer it. If you are driving to New York by car and you see a signpost with "New York" on it, your presupposition is that that road will lead to New York and so you go that way. You take it for granted.

Most presuppositions in our daily lives are unproblematic and sufficiently reliable. They are functional; they regulate our actions. However, there are also presuppositions that are incorrect or at least wrongly taken to be true. When your colleague shouts, "Enough said. Now action!", he presupposes that talking is not action. This proposition must be understood to be true (by the speaker) in order to make sense of this sentence. Otherwise the speaker would be talking nonsense. Therefore it is a presupposition. But it is a problematic one because it's incorrect. Talking may be a different kind of action from walking or cycling but it is an activity!

You master the technique of critical thinking when you can recognize and question those assumptions or presuppositions. In the pub, Peter's assumption that Nancy is someone who's having loud parties every weekend turned out, after investigation, to be questionable. It could very well have been just this once. And if Nancy keeps quiet indoors too, Peter might even accept that she could stay in the neighborhood—and, who knows, they might even become friends!

Simple basic exercise in critical thinking: Plato's cave—musical chairs

This exercise on arguing is a playful and very low-threshold "doing" exercise. It is suitable for a group of children or young people who like to play. It is also an introductory exercise. The participants learn the basics: how to express a point of view, how to distinguish between a point of view and an argument, how to give an argument, how to question an argument.

The exercise is called 'Plato's cave' because it focuses on the distinction between the world of visible things and that of invisible things. You can also introduce the exercise by telling the story of Plato's cave very briefly. It can then function, for example, as a first introduction to the world of philosophy.

Target group
The exercise is suitable for groups of up to 30 and can be played from the age of 6.

Objectives
The participants:

- playfully learn the difference between the world of visible, tangible, everyday things and the world of ideas, as expressed in conceptions;
- get to know each other better in the process.

Specific objectives from the list: Po2 + Po3 + Po5 + Po8 + Po11 + T1 + T5 + T21 + Pe1 + Pe2 + Pe6 + Pe7 + Pe11

Time and supplies
Minimum 15 minutes, no maximum. A circle of chairs. There is one chair less than the number of participants. It is important that there is enough space around the circle to allow movement.

Activity
The group sits in a circle on the chairs, one of which is missing. Someone stands in the middle and formulates a statement, for example: "Anyone who wears laces in their shoes must change seats." Whoever meets this criterion (round 1 or 2) or agrees with the statement (round 3) has to find another seat as quickly as possible. The speaker in the middle must also find a seat as soon as possible after speaking. The slowest participant has to come and stand in the middle and answer the next criterion.

There are three rounds:

- First round (at the front of the cave): only things that are visible here and now (e.g. "Everyone with black trousers must change places").

- Second round (a little further back in the cave): only things that you can observe, but not necessarily here and now (e.g. "Everyone who has a sister at home must change places"). Here it is important that everyone is honest.
- Third round (at the back of the cave): only invisible things, opinions (e.g. "Anyone who thinks that God exists must change places").

In the third round, there is the variation "argument butterfly." Here, someone goes out of the circle, and when he taps on the shoulder of a participant, that person has to give a single argument to justify why he/she stayed in place or didn't stay. If he taps twice, the person has to give two arguments, and so on.

There is also the variation "question butterfly." Here, a second person leaves the circle. When this butterfly taps someone's shoulder (after the arguing butterfly has tapped), this person may ask up to three questions with the aim of making the arguer think about his/her arguments.

5. The Performance

There is a jam session in which Ionica Minune plays together with the ensemble Kaliakra.[11]

Here you see six men full of positive energy. They are having fun. And if you look closely, you can see that not only are the musicians laughing but the audience is having fun as well. The energy is overwhelming.

They are "in the flow," as it is called. Light as this may seem, the music is virtuosic. It sounds a piece of cake, but just try playing it! This is technical mastery at its best. One super-fast solo follows after another and, as is also the case in jazz, this is only possible when the musicians are well attuned to each other. They concentrate on what they are here for—making music together. They are constantly focused on something other than themselves. As individuals, they don't get in the way of the beauty of their production.

Listen to the beginning. During the initial introduction, the musicians smile at each other and wait as they look at Minune, the leader of the group. Only when he starts the melody do the others follow. That he is the leader is not so obvious. Occasionally, someone takes the lead and the rhythms vary, but never at the expense of the collective harmony. Minune does not apparently assert himself as a leader. But you can see his leadership in the look he gives his friends when he indicates that they can begin or end a solo.

Here you see a bandleader who does not say how something should be played. He just does it. He shows it constantly. And he does it with a lightness and naturalness. A real maestro. The attitude and technique are there. Next, the performance. It has to be light and correct. With an audience! The "notes" in a philosophical conversation are the questions and answers from the participants. They must be correctly formulated and to the point. They have to steer the conversation in the right direction. If you are a facilitator, you usually do not answer, just like the conductor who doesn't play music himself. But you are responsible for making the music happen. You do this by asking questions. Or by remaining silent. If a participant asks you a question, you only answer when your intervention does not interfere with the participant's thought process. You are the facilitator, so you don't have to think—at least not about the content. That will come naturally. According to what you do or don't do, you are at all times a model for the participants. So when they give their opinion and their arguments, they do so as briefly and to the point as you yourself. The same goes for the questions they ask. By doing it well, they slowly but surely take over the role and place of the facilitator, until eventually they can do it autonomously, as in the music fragment. Then, as the facilitator, you can look around satisfied and drink some coffee.

If you are hesitant about leading such a conversation "out of the blue," the score will fortunately give you something to hold on to. In this part about the "performance," initially you will find a few competencies that form the basis of the concert. It can be summarized as speaking clearly and asking good questions. Only when you have mastered these basic skills can you make the "five movements" smoothly. These movements are, in fact, the conductor's gestures. They determine the harmony of the conversation. The interplay between these movements is the symphony—literally: how it sounds as a whole. A good facilitator knows which movement to make at which moment and with which question. When the participants (musicians) perform this, they show their skill. They show how their formed critical minds express themselves in what they say as they respond to the facilitator's questions.

Of course, you can read a lot about how a successful performance should sound. Even better is to listen to one. In the second part of this chapter, you can listen to such a performance and observe the movements. A group of children talk about dancing animals. But we are not there yet. First we have to learn to play some notes correctly and practice some scales before the real work starts.

5.1. The foundation

Doh–re–mi–fah–sol. Sing clearly. Every note the same length. Then a little faster. Shorter notes. This is the beginning of the music lesson. This is the basis of a conversation—just being able to say something clearly and ask a question. How simple can it be?

5.1.1. Speaking briefly and to the point

When I hear all this from the neighborhood and so on, I have the feeling that there is something wrong here.

Problem number one. You have finally met Nancy two streets away from the pub. But how this woman speaks! She is verbose. You can certainly cut out half the words here without losing meaning. So you ask her: "Can you say this in eight words?" This discipline in the number of words sounds very strict. Nancy is startled. But it works very well. By imposing a form on her, you help her to structure her thinking. She says: "I don't feel welcome here." That's much better.

Problem number two. You probably know someone who enjoys talking for a long time. Let's call him "Henry." Acting as he does, Henry doesn't realize how much listening is required from you. Henry wants to be heard but does not listen well himself. When his monologue is over, you can ask: "Could you summarize this in a maximum of three sentences?" In a group, you can let others ask that as well, or you can make the suggestion yourself. If he agrees to offer a shorter version, then the next question is obvious: "Why previously did you need to say it at such length?" That comes over as a little terse. But if you think he needs this kind of treatment, why not do it? Next time, Henry will learn to be more concise. In this way he will become a better interlocutor for himself and the others. He will be grateful to you!

Problem number three. A participant does not express himself adequately because there is a contradiction between his words and his behavior (number 2 in the score under "performance"). An example:

> **Facilitator:** What do you think about that, Yvan?
> **Yvan:** (Sighs, throws up his eyes.) What am I thinking? I guess it's not important, is it?

First of all, it is noticeable that Yvan repeats the facilitator's question. This may mean that he wants to check his own understanding of the question. But if it happens systematically and regularly, it may also indicate a resistance to the facilitator. After all, by repeating the question, Yvan becomes the authority, and not the facilitator. He then only answers the questions he formulates himself. If it is a problem for the group or for himself, you can raise it:

> **Facilitator:** Why do you keep repeating my question before you answer it, Yvan?

This is putting him on the spot, of course. Yvan will have to explain his attitude, but this can be useful. It can teach him to "play the game" again and do it better.

There is a second problem with Yvan's intervention. Indirectly he gives other signals with his body language. The interpretation of this is difficult because we are not Yvan. Presumably, he wants confirmation here. He wants the facilitator to say: "Of course, Yvan, that's important!" But in a philosophical conversation, expressing oneself adequately is an exercise for each participant. The facilitator does not deprive the participant of any opportunity to practice this, not even by giving him the confirmation he seeks. So you ask a question:

Facilitator: Why do you think that's not important now, Yvan?

Now Yvan can pull himself together and express what he really wants to say. He will also take responsibility for the process; he will have to explain his point to the others.

As well as giving concise answers, asking questions is no easy task. The trick is to ask the right question, on the right topic, with the right words at the right time and to the right person. An intervention such as "When I hear that, I wonder if it's alright for you" is not as good as "Is it alright for you?" After all, the former is simply not a question. Just as a correctly played note is the hallmark of a good musician, a well-formulated question is also the hallmark of a good facilitator. Below, you will find ten short tips. They're the basis of good questioning. If you learn them by heart and then apply them daily, you will not only become a better conversationalist and facilitator but it will also dramatically change your social life. Good luck!

5.1.2. Asking questions: ten golden tips

1. Formulate one question at a time

It's Sunday morning. Mum asks her 16-year-old daughter: "So, how was the party yesterday? Were there a lot of people? Did you have a good time? Did you see Sandy?"

The daughter is silent, scratches her head, and goes on Instagramming. What do you expect? If you ask many questions at once, you are actually busy with your own thinking. You are not paying attention to the other person! One question at a time allows you to pay more attention to the other person's reaction.

2. Formulate your question as simply as possible

When you ask a question, your intention is that the participant thinks about the answer and not about the question. If your question is too difficult or too vaguely formulated, he will not understand you. Try to formulate your question as simply as possible. A philosophical discussion is difficult enough for the participants! So, instead of "Would it be possible to test this out empirically?", just ask "Can you give an example of this?"

3. Formulate your question as briefly as possible

A characteristic of a well-formulated question is that the participant remembers the question. A question like "What is your responsibility as a parent given the fact that you are in charge of two adolescents who are struggling to find their own way in life?" is difficult to reproduce by the interlocutor. He has to forget much of it. So it is better to ask, "What is your responsibility as a parent of two adolescents?" A good maximum is about ten words.

4. Do not introduce new concepts

Just as a chameleon sitting in a tree takes on the colors of the tree and becomes invisible to enemies, a good questioner uses the participant's words as much as possible. In this way, the participant can recognize himself in the question and will be more readily motivated to answer it. If you copy the words, it is a sign that you have listened well. Besides this psychological advantage, there is also a cognitive advantage: your participant can concentrate better. He will not be distracted by new concepts. So the facilitator has fewer distractions. He continues to listen alertly and is not waylaid by his own thinking.

An example:

Participant: I am afraid to stand up for myself.
Non-chameleon facilitator: What is the cause of this fear?
Chameleon facilitator: Why are you afraid?

5. Ask open questions
An open question is a question where the other person feels free to answer anything. A closed question is a question where the other person feels pushed in a certain direction.

An open question is, for example, "What do you think of this training?" The closed variant is: "This training is boring, isn't it?"

A closed question can also be called a "suggestive" or "rhetorical" question. These questions do have advantages. They enable you to win people over to your side. After such a rhetorical question as "Right?", you are no longer alone. You are supported. An open question is much more "lonely." The chance is about 50 percent that you will have people who will answer something you like. But they will answer what they think and not what you want them to think.

6. Listen more than you talk
The art of asking questions is the same as the art of listening. A well-formulated question is the result of careful listening to the other person. Listening means above all being silent,

as you read in Chapter 3. Only in your silence can the other person reveal himself as another person and develop his ideas. The silence implies the acceptance of every sentence the other person will produce, and also the realization that it will always be different from what you think. Through this silence the other person will feel respected. Only under this condition can you work productively with the thinking of the other person.

7. Be alert and free in your questioning

Suppose a participant says: "Yes, it is very sensitive, you know?" Here, as a questioner, you may be tempted to sympathize rather than ask a question. Or you may start to doubt the question you would like to ask because it might harm the participant. If this doubt is caused by your fear, for example of hurting the participant, it is not necessary to give in to this doubt. However, if you believe that the appropriateness of your intervention should be taken into account in light of the process, you should not ignore it. It is a subtle difference, but someone who engages in philosophical conversations as facilitator has the state of mind of a child. He has no intention to hurt. He is morally, socially, and politically neutral when listing to his participants.

8. Provide emotional comfort for your participant

Whatever you want to achieve with your questions (reflection, support, clarification, and so on), it is important that the participant is central to the process and not you. There must be freedom for him to answer. He will not feel this freedom if he is under stress or pressure, if you dominate him, or make him afraid. If this were so, then he would do what you want by force or out of obedience. He would not feel that he was the one central to the process.

You make your participant feel at ease by having an open, inviting attitude. He needs to feel that he is a person who is accepted. The more you can enable this emotional support, the further you can take your questioning. We can compare a counselor to a doctor. The more emotional resistance the patient offers, the more difficult it will be to achieve the desired medical outcome. If your participant surrenders to you on the basis of emotional acceptance, you will be able to make more far-reaching interventions in what he says and thinks.

9. Respect your own question

Often a participant reacts to a question instead of answering it. He associates words in the question with his own concepts or interprets them in a different direction than intended.

For example:

Facilitator: How did you enjoy your further education?
Participant: It's not easy to get into further education — you have to have enough qualifications.

Maybe the participant will make a digression and come back to the question later. Are you going to wait for that? You have to choose here. You can let your participant set the rules of the game. If you do that, the way you formulate a question, carefully or not, does not strictly matter. The other person will go their own way and you will end up talking about what they have decided is relevant. In daily life, this happens often and it is not a problem. It is just important that you realize that it happens and that you allow it to happen.

If, on the other hand, you decide to steer your interlocutor into talking about the desired subject, other interventions are necessary. The simplest thing is to interrupt him and repeat your question: "I just wanted to know how you enjoyed your further education?" You can do this once or twice or even three times. If the other person still does not answer your question, it is time to tackle this behavior. You can do this, for example, with a question like "Why don't you answer my question, even though I've repeated it three times?"

10. Think carefully about introductions to questions

A well-formulated question, addressed to the right person on the right subject at the right time, can work wonders. To accomplish this, such a question must be bare, stripped of unnecessary words. So try to avoid introductions like "What I would like to ask you is..." or "I have always wondered..." These are simply not questions; they are announcements, personal messages, and so on. So the other person doesn't have to answer. He will probably say "Good for you" or something like that.

Any introduction to a question is therefore superfluous. You may have a tendency to repeat something about the other person before you ask your question, for example: "I heard you say that you don't need a lot of money to be happy. Are you saying that...?" Such an introduction usually serves to reassure the questioner himself that he has heard the participant correctly. It is not always necessary for the participant himself.

Is an introduction, then, never OK? If you know that you are going to ask a controversial question, an introduction may be a good thing as a "lubricant" for your question. An introduction such as "You may feel a little shocked by what I am about to ask you, but..." provides emotional support for a question about which a participant may be a little tense. But even then it is up to him to accept this question or not. An introduction is also functional if you want to make the interlocutor aware of what he has already said, or if you want to introduce him to a hypothetical situation.

5.2. The performance: the five movements

The pleasure and enjoyment of the philosophical conversation is the fruit of technical mastery and concentration. Only in this way can you get the most out of it and, moreover, there is room for improvisation. Just listen to how it goes in a class of a dozen 10-year-olds. They are sitting together to have a philosophical conversation under the guidance of a philosopher. We stay in the mood, because we are talking about…dancing.

5.2.1. Can animals dance?

The children sit in a circle. They have just seen a clip from the Walt Disney film *Jungle Book*. It is the fragment in which Baloo the bear dances. Laughter. The question that arose: can animals dance?

1. **Facilitator (F):** So, can animals dance?
2. (Meryem raises her hand.)
3. **F:** Yes, Meryem, tell me.
4. **Meryem:** I don't know.
5. **F:** What do you think? Yes or no?
6. **Meryem:** Well, no, I don't think animals really know music.

Meryem wants to join in. She raises her hand. But she hesitates to play the first note, in other words, answer the question. That is why the facilitator makes a first move. He encourages her to play, even if it is out of tune or has nothing to do with the issue—a first note is a first note!

At the beginning, the participants commit themselves to the game. They make themselves ready to address the question. Gyorgei has less difficulty with this than Meryem.

7. **Gyorgei:** Yes, they can dance. We have a parrot at home and every time the radio is on, he does this… (Gyorgei moves his head forwards and backwards.)
8. **F:** OK, Gyorgei, but why do you think that is dancing?
9. **Gyorgei:** Well, the parrot moves rhythmically to music and that's dancing, isn't it?

Here we have Gyorgei's solo: he immediately provides an anecdote, an example, with his answer. One example is not enough to substantiate his statement that "animals can dance," but it is a start! And that is why the teacher asks him to elaborate; he asks him to connect this anecdote with an argument by asking him why he thinks that what the parrot does can be called dancing. He immediately gets an argument from Gyorgei: the parrot dances because it moves rhythmically to music. Straight away there is a reaction to this from another child in the group.

> 10. **Yorik:** Not true. Soldiers also move rhythmically to music, but that is not dancing; that is marching.
> 11. **F:** OK, so what's the difference between dancing and marching?
> 12. **Yorik:** I don't know.

There is now some pace in this performance. We already have a counter-example. Now we have to compare the concepts of "dancing" and "marching," because although both are "rhythmic movement to music," they have different names. So there must be a difference. Fortunately, others enter the stage to explain this further.

> 13. **Maggie:** Marching, that's something you learn when you join the army. Dancing is not the same; you don't have to learn it.
> 14. **Cyrille:** No, my mum and my dad go to a dance class every Thursday evening. They're learning to dance there.
> 15. **F:** Catherine, can you repeat what the difference is between what Cyrille says and what Maggie says about dancing?
> 16. **Catherine:** Maggie says that you cannot teach dancing like marching, and Cyrille says that you can because his mum and dad are learning it in the dance school.
> 17. **F:** That's right?

18. (Cyrille and Maggie nod.)

19. **F:** So do we have an agreement that you can teach both?

20. (The participants nod.)

Just like in an orchestra, you cannot play well (solo) if you don't listen to the others. It is Catherine who has been listening to what the others have been saying. After she has expressed this so well, we can agree on something. We have an agreement! But we are not finished yet…

21. **F:** So what's the difference between marching and dancing?

22. **Len:** (Intervening.) In the army you have to march on command. The general or something like that then shouts "To march, march!" or something like that. (He does this.) With dancing, it is not like that. You can't dance on command. Dancing is spontaneous.

23. **Miguel:** Yes, but I can also march spontaneously. Watch! (He starts marching in the middle of the circle.)

24. **F:** Why do you call that spontaneous?

25. **Miguel:** Just because…I just do it; I don't think about it.

26. **F:** In your opinion, then, is doing something "spontaneously" the same as "just" doing something and doing something "without thinking"?

27. **Miguel:** Yes!

28. **F:** And why is that not on command?

29. **Miguel:** Well, nobody asked me, did they? Then I would have to think about it. In this case it was spontaneous.

30. (Others nod.)

Here the facilitator asks Miguel to explain why his example, his own marching, is not on command. He uses three different concepts in his explanation: "spontaneous," "just doing," and "doing something without thinking." All three are equal according to him.

The facilitator can sidetrack and ask the others if that is correct. For example, he can ask, "Does anyone have an example of something you do spontaneously and which is *not* without thinking?"

Just like in jazz music, sidetracks are always possible. However, because he feels that would lead the discussion too far from the main theme, he returns to it.

31. **F:** Len, can you tell me what we agreed when it comes to the difference between dancing and marching?

32. **Len:** I think we said that you can do both dancing and marching spontaneously. But you can also learn both. You can do both.

33. **F:** What about that commanding thing?

34. **Len:** I think you can order someone to march, but you can't order them to dance.

35. **Catherine:** I don't agree with that. You have those dancers in bars and so on who dance on "orders" from their boss. That may not be fun to do, but it is possible.

36. **F:** And is it therefore no longer spontaneous?

37. **Catherine:** No, because the boss asks them to. They don't do it on their own initiative.

38. **F:** What do you think of that, Len?

39. **Len:** OK, yes, you can dance on command.

40. **F:** So is that not a point of difference?

41. (They shake their heads.)

We are in the middle of the musical piece. The participants explore different characteristics of dancing by comparing it with another similar activity. The counter-example is surprising. Yes, indeed, you can also dance on command. And yes, indeed, you can also march spontaneously! The new perspectives on the theme contribute to the fun in the game. It is exciting! But in the meantime we have lost sight of the parrot. So it is time for the supervisor to return to an earlier part of the process.

42. **F:** OK. So does Gyorgei's parrot dance or march or something else?

43. **Len:** At least he doesn't do it on command; he does it spontaneously.

44. **Gyorgei:** I don't know about that. We bought him from someone else. Maybe that previous owner taught him that.

45. **Miguel:** But it's not because he learned it that he can't be spontaneous. We just said that. I think it's both.

46. **Gyorgei:** Yes, that is true.

47. **F:** OK, but is it marching or dancing that the parrot does?

48. **Miguel:** It's not marching, because he stays on his perch and he only moves his head.

49. **F:** And is it dancing?

50. **Gyorgei:** He moves rhythmically to the music, but only with his head.

The participants now study the question of the parrot in more detail. And this poses a new problem: is it enough to move only your head and still be deemed to be dancing?

At this point, the timid Meryem, who spoke briefly at the beginning, makes a comeback and takes a completely different tack.

51. **Meryem:** I don't know. I think animals just don't hear music.

52. **F:** Why, Meryem?

53. **Meryem:** Well, animals don't sing along and so on, do they? I think they only hear sounds, but no music.

54. **Catherine:** OK, but I think they do hear a rhythm. At home, when the music is loud and I dance to it, my dog dances along. It's very funny to see!

55. **F:** What does he do? Can you show me?

56. (Catherine stands up and shakes her body back and forth.)

57. **F:** What do we think about this? Do you think Catherine's little dog dances?

58. **Yorik:** I don't believe it. The dog is just moving with you because you are dancing.

59. **Catherine:** What's the difference?

60. **F:** Sarah, can you explain the difference to Catherine?

61. **Sarah:** (Speaking for the first time—very quietly and hesitantly.) I don't know.

62. **F:** Who can help Sarah? Gyorgei, you are sitting next to her. Do you know the difference?

63. **Gyorgei:** Yes.

64. **F:** Can you explain it to Sarah then? (Gyorgei does so, whispering in her ear.)

65. **F:** Can you put it into words now, Sarah?

66. **Sarah:** Yorik says that the dog does not hear the music but just moves along with Catherine, and Catherine says that he dances to the music.

Here, the "maître d'orchestre" engages a new player. He asks her to lend a hand so that she can play the first note. It starts easily: she just has to repeat what Gyorgei whispers to her. This plenary formulation is a first step in the philosophical conversation. It is by no means self-evident for any participant; you have to learn it. Now that Sarah is playing along, it is her turn to take a position! The facilitator encourages her as follows.

67. **F:** OK, Sarah. And what do you think of that yourself?

68. **Sarah:** I don't know.

69. **F:** What are you unsure about?

70. **Sarah:** I don't know if dogs can hear music.

71. **F:** What do you think? Yes or no?

72. **Sarah:** Well, they probably hear the sounds and the rhythm. And some animals might move in response to that and others not. A cow for example doesn't do that!

73. (The participants laugh, and so does the facilitator.)

Our new musician (Sarah) brings a whole new and cheerful note to the ensemble. It took a while and some doubts had to be removed. But a new sound emerged. It still sounds high; it still hangs in the air. It still has to be brought "down to earth" — to Catherine's small dog. Sarah has yet to speak about that.

> 74. **F:** OK, great. So what does that mean for that dog of Catherine's?
> 75. **Sarah:** I think he moves along with Catherine, and therefore a bit to that rhythm.
> 76. **F:** But would you say that he dances?
> 77. **Sarah:** No, I wouldn't.
> 78. **F:** Anyone else who thinks that?
> 79. **F:** Who can explain why not?
> 80. **Cyrille:** I believe what Catherine says — that the dog moves along to the sound. He is not going to do that on his own. He moves along with his owner.
> 81. **F:** Is that right, Catherine? Doesn't he do that on his own?
> 82. **Catherine:** No, I don't think so. But I'm not really sure. I wouldn't be there when he does it on his own, would I?
> 83. (Everyone laughs.)

We are approaching an intermediate cadence in the piece here, although we are not quite sure. It looks as if the little dog does not dance, but only moves along to the sound. But isn't the latter also a dance? Now that we have a second animal example with the dog, we can compare the parrot and the dog.

> 84. **F:** OK. And what's the difference between what the dog does and what the parrot does?
> 85. **Cyrille:** Well, the parrot does that on its own when the music is on. The dog doesn't.
> 86. **F:** Is there any other difference?

87. **Cyrille:** Well, the dog also dances with his legs, the parrot only with its head.

88. **F:** And is one more like dancing than the other, or not?

89. **Cyrille:** I don't know.

90. **F:** OK. I'll just put some music on now. (The facilitator puts a rhythmic song on his smartphone.) Now move to the music like the parrot: only with your head.

91. (The participants do this, for just half a minute.)

92. **F:** OK. Would you call what you have done now "dancing"?

93. **Catherine:** No, it is moving with the music, but to speak of dancing you also have to move your legs.

94. **F:** So if a bird like that parrot also moved its legs, it would be dancing?

95. **Catherine:** Yes, I think so. My dog did that too.

96. **F:** And does it matter if you move with me, for example, or if you do it on your own like the parrot?

97. **Catherine:** No, it makes no difference; in both cases it's dancing.

98. **F:** What do the rest of you think?

5.2.2. The guidance of the five movements

You can see here the deliberately "non-knowing" attitude of the facilitator in practice (Po4 in the score). He doesn't give his opinion about what is dancing or not. He is the midwife of the thoughts. His task is to give birth to the insights the participants are pregnant with. His job is not to add insights. He has a neutral attitude towards the content. In a sense, he does not care what dancing really is. His task is to intensify the research of the participants.

What questions does he use to do this? And what is the purpose of those questions? How is that piece of "music" put together? We distinguish a few essential "movements" here that form the core of the conversation. In itself, it is not important which question the facilitator asks at any moment. Just as in Minune's band, playing different notes from those written on paper is not a problem. In fact, there is no paper at all in Minune's band.

More important than the right words is that you, as a facilitator, trigger a certain movement in the participants' thinking. These movements and the interplay between them form the core of the philosophical conversation. They are the harmony of the musical piece. Without harmony, they are loose, incoherent notes. Without these five movements, the philosophical conversation is a chatty get-together or a ship lost at sea. So read carefully what is written below and learn the points by heart.

The basic movements in a philosophical conversation, which can also be found in the score (at the beginning of the book), are the following.

1. To position

Everything that the participants say in a conversation can be seen as the notes of a piece of music. The conductor is looking for a root note in all these notes, a chord, on which to work further. The motor in a philosophical conversation is an opinion. We need a participant who has an opinion about something. Whoever expresses an opinion *positions* himself. Gyorgei does this, for example, by saying that animals can dance (line 7). The facilitator hears this. It is an important chord in the piece of music. He can then ask others to position themselves against it or to share this position. Some take up positions spontaneously. With other participants, you have to ask for it. For example, the facilitator does this when he asks Sarah: "Would you say that he (Catherine's dog) dances?" (line 76).

There are two kinds of position: general and concrete. Gyorgei takes a position, but it is still a general statement. It has yet to be tested against reality. When Sarah says that the

77

dog does not dance (line 77), she is taking a position on the starting question, but it is not yet about animals in general, only about the dog. It is a concrete statement. That, in turn, must be tested against the theory by comparing the little dog with other animals.

Like playing a chord in an orchestra, taking a position is risky. You get a bit exposed by revealing your answer to the question. This move can be useful with participants who are a little shy or who may lack self-confidence, like Sarah here. It can also be helpful with participants who say something that you suspect they do not mean or who are being ironic. For example, suppose someone says in an exaggerated tone: "*Yes that is really very well done!*" The facilitator then asks: "So, you say that it's well done?" By taking these words seriously in his tone, the facilitator immediately neutralizes the irony and leads the participant to take a position that he/she really supports. So, positioning involves the participants saying what they authentically, really mean at a given moment. It also involves doing this in a way that is understandable to others. For example, if a participant's story is unclear and long, the facilitator can always ask: "Can you say it more concisely?"

2. To argue

When Miguel (with great success in the class) starts marching and calls it "spontaneous," the facilitator draws attention to how Miguel gives his opinion that marching is also spontaneous. However, no argument has been given as to why it should be spontaneous, so the facilitator asks the question: "Why do you call that spontaneous?" (line 24). Then Miguel gives a general argument. He has to explain what "spontaneous" is and what the difference is between that and "being commanded." You can also argue with a factual argument, or an observation argument. This happens, for example, when Cyrille says that his mum and dad have dancing lessons (line 14). He then gives an observation that serves as a counter-argument to the point of view that you cannot teach dancing. When Cyrille compares the dancing of the dog and of the parrot, he also gives an observation argument (line 87): the dog dances with its legs and the parrot does not. It is an argument because it functions as part of a reasoning process. So, if the speaker thinks that dancing involves using the legs, it follows that the parrot does not dance and the dog does.

The reasoning is as follows:

General argument (concealed): Dancing requires you to move your legs.
Factual argument: The parrot dances without moving its legs.
Conclusion: The parrot does not dance.

Another observation argument was that the parrot dances alone and the little dog moves together with a person (line 80). The reasoning behind this is as follows:

General argument (concealed): If you only move together with another person and cannot do so on your own, that is not dancing.
Factual argument: The dog only moves with Catherine and cannot do so on its own.
Conclusion: The dog does not dance.

But this is not yet a consensus. What still needs to be investigated further is:

• The perception argument. Are we sure that the little dog cannot do that on its own? Catherine says she is not sure.
• The general argument: whether it is necessary that you can at least do that by yourself.

3. To concretize/to abstract

After Catherine has claimed that her dog dances with her, the facilitator asks: "What does he do? Can you show me?" (line 55). He asks here for concreteness. He is asking a *question downwards*, about the perception on which her position is based. You can also *ask upwards*, about the ideas or the concept that lies behind the statement. When Catherine talks about dancers who have to dance on orders from the boss, the facilitator asks: "And is it therefore no longer spontaneous?" (line 36). He is asking for an opinion on this example.

The philosophical conversation alternates between downward questions concerning the perception of events and upward questions concerning thinking. Downward questions include "Where was that?" or "How many people were there?" as well as questions about private experiences, such as "What went through your mind at the time?" or "How did you experience that?" Upward questions include "Why was that?" or "How do you explain that?" but also "What do they have to do with each other?" or "Why is that true?" To lead a conversation is a constant combination of upward and downward questions.

With young children, it sometimes happens that one story provokes another and many stories are told associatively so that after a while they lose sight of the link with the question or issue. Then a question like "What does that have to do with happiness?" is a good move. The other way round is even more common: the conversation becomes abstract because only concepts and reasoning are exchanged. Or stories may be told, but in abstract terms such as "What I often experience is…" Here a downward question is appropriate: "OK, when was the last time you experienced this?"

Concretization gives a philosophical conversation flesh and blood. When the participants talk here about dancing with the legs versus with the head (line 87), the facilitator even introduces a here-and-now experience by way of concretization. He offers them the opportunity to experience it at first hand and then to make the link with the reasoning again. This is actually what a scientist does all the time: a hypothesis (you can dance with your head as well as with your legs separately) is tested here against an experience (if I only move with my head, I don't call that dancing) in order subsequently to adjust the hypothesis and thereby also improve the theory.

The facilitator can do that because he does not take a position on the content. He offers an extra experience that makes the investigation not only richer but also more vivid and fun. The same happens when he asks Catherine to show him how the dog moves (line 55). This makes it immediately clear whether this is dancing or not.

This emphasis on concreteness in the philosophical conversation is an inheritance from Germany, more specifically from the Walkemühle in Adelshausen. This was not only a primary school but also a people's college founded in the early 1920s by teacher Ludwig Wunder—the name appeals to the imagination—and his philosophy professor, Leonard Nelson.[12] Nelson was a philosopher who placed great importance on independent, critical thinking. He had already started experimenting with the "Socratic method" in his philosophy classes.[13] Nelson believed that it should be possible, as in Plato's texts describing Socrates' efforts, to gain insight into an idea through conversation. And this had to happen through rigorous, careful, and critical reflection on the experience. So the language used had to be concrete, as close to the facts as possible. According to Nelson, the task of the philosophy teacher is to teach pupils to speak and think clearly and concretely, with German *Gründlichkeit!*[14] In his essay 'The Socratic Method' from 1922 he writes about this:

...the philosophy adept hates nothing so much as the concrete use of his mind, a use that is directed towards the assessment of facts and that therefore forces him to remember the lower-order instruments of his five senses. Ask someone in a philosophy exercise "What do you see on the board?" You can be sure that he will lower his gaze to the ground, and after repeating the question, "What do you see on the board?" he will force out a sentence beginning with "if," thus indicating that the world of facts does not exist for him.

4. To listen

Just like in Minune's orchestra, in a philosophical conversation many things happen at the same time. There is not only the concentration on what you yourself bring to the table: the position, examples, or arguments. There is also concentration on what the other person is saying and on what you are saying. Listening manifests itself in the ability to repeat verbatim what you have said yourself or what someone else has said. The facilitator can do that too: he remembers everything literally as it was said. But he also asks this of his participants. The facilitator can use a listening movement:

- If a participant uses confused language, he can ask the participant to repeat what he has said so that it becomes clearer. The clearer expression of what the participant was saying then becomes "positioning." What preceded it was "listening," but to himself.
- To involve a group member in the discussion.
- To get someone out of his urge to manifest his thoughts and bring something into the discussion himself. By asking such a participant to first repeat what someone else has said, he also concentrates on the group.
- To reinforce an anchor point in the conversation (a point on which they agree).

Here in the conversation, the facilitator explicitly invites Catherine to contribute at one point. For example, he asks her to repeat the two positions of Maggie and Cyrille (line 15). A little later, he asks Len to articulate what the group agrees on (line 31). Such a listening movement is a resting point for the other participants in the conversation. In general, this slows down the pace and is therefore especially appropriate when the conversation takes on the character of a heated discussion or when the conversation speeds up.

Listening is a function of thinking in a group. Professor Matthew Lipman, who with Ann Margaret Sharp started the tradition of 'P4C' (philosophy for children) in New York in the early 1970s, called such a discussion group the 'Community of Philosophical Inquiry' (abbreviated as CoPI). The CoPI is a kind of mini-democracy in which the pupils grow in self-confidence and learn to deal with differences of opinion. The teacher is not an authoritarian figure here, but a discussion partner who fuels inquiry.[15] This group was also a function of knowledge building. Lipman's philosophy was influenced by John Dewey. According to Dewey, knowledge is social and is created in constant interaction with the world—people solve problems together on a daily basis. This is already the case in human evolution, but it is also the case in philosophy and science: problems are identified, hypotheses are formulated (ideas, concepts, theories), and people then act according to the best solution. This happens best in such a democratic discussion group, where participants interact on an equal footing. It is in the practice of this democratic dialogical activity itself that more efficient knowledge emerges.[16]

5. To investigate

The movement of inquiries happens when different points of view and arguments are on the table. Then the question is: who is right—which reasoning or argument is stronger than another?

As a group, one has to come to a conclusion. For example, at a certain moment Len is busy comparing the three criteria for dancing: spontaneous, learned, on command (lines 32, 34). Because of this research and Catherine's counter-example, Len realizes that you can also dance on command, so that is not where the difference lies (line 39). In the mind of such a participant, a comparison therefore takes place.

On the question of whether the parrot is spontaneous, Gyorgei raises doubts: the movement could also have been learned from the previous owner (line 44). He formulates a hypothesis here. He then examines the causal relationship: if it is learned, does that mean it is not spontaneous? Through Miguel, who repeats this observation, Gyorgei applies this principle here and deductively concludes that one does not exclude the other (lines 45–46).

After Catherine imitates the behavior of the little dog, the participants analyze this behavior to see if it is about just moving together with someone or dancing (line 58). And when they all move together like the parrot to the music, Catherine analyzes this experience. She concludes that, in order to speak of dancing, you also have to move your legs (lines 93–95).

5.2.3. Difficult groups do not exist

Look again at the Minune orchestra at the end of this chapter. If you pay attention to how they look, you will see aspects of what we called "attitude" in Chapter 3. You see the listening, the sitting still, the alertness, the regard, the focus on something other than themselves. The technique of playing is so well mastered that everyone's full concentration can go into the performance. It is controlled; it happens automatically. The performance is only the externalization of attitude and technique.

The movements you read above are automatic in a conversation once the posture and technique have been learned. When you have mastered them, you can perform them in any context, with any group. There are no difficult groups for a master who knows his score inside out. But the facilitator has to make a start somewhere as an accompanist. You can read how to do this in the next chapter.

Exercise: Socrates at the marketplace

This exercise can be used as a "philosophical introduction." It allows the participants to hear each other speak in a safe one-to-one setting. But it also allows them to get to know each other in their ability to ask questions and to continue to ask questions. It is also an exercise in "maieutics": you practice the attitude of the midwife of thoughts.

Objectives and target group
The exercise is suitable for small and large groups of participants and can be performed from the age of 10, but is more suitable for young people and adults than for children. It is helpful if there is an even number of participants. If this is not the case, then appoint someone as "butterfly" for each round. This person's task is to check with each group to see if everyone is following the instructions.

Specific objectives from the score : Po2 + Po3 + Po4 + Po5 + Po6 + Po8 + Po11 + T1 + T2 + T5 + T17 + T19 + T20 + Pe1 + Pe6 + Pe7 + Pe8 + Pe9 + Pe10 + Pe11

Time and supplies
The exercise takes about an hour. The instructions and the run-up at the beginning take about 10 minutes. Then there are three rounds of 2 x 3 minutes with some preliminary and follow-up discussion. All in all, 10 minutes per round.

The requirements are a large room, a notebook for each participant, something to write with, and a set of blank cards. Also a timer/smartphone and a bell.

Activity

a) You can introduce the exercise by telling something about Socrates: a person who pestered people in the marketplace / public spaces with questions in order to get them to think about what they themselves thought was important. You can also talk about the "midwife" idea. This exercise requires a similar attitude from the questioners.

b) Each participant writes down a question in their notebook. It should be a question that he or she would like to have answered at this moment in his or her life or work. It is important that it is a "real" question, not a "game" question. It may be a very practical question, e.g. "Should I buy a new car?" or a "bigger" question like "Should I change partners?" It is of no further importance.

c) The facilitator gives some instructions to improve this first formulation of the question:

   i. Make the question as short as possible.

   ii. Make sure it is open-ended: there should be no hidden answers (for example, not "Don't you think young people spend too much time on their cellphones?").

   iii. Formulate the question in such a way that someone who knows nothing about your life or work can still give a meaningful answer without having to request additional information. In other words, formulate the question as generally as possible. (For example, if your question is: "What shall I feed my cat tonight?" then it is impossible for someone else to give a meaningful answer without additional information. So it is better to say: "Does it matter what you give to cats to eat?")

iv. Formulate the question as simply as possible. When someone hears the question, they understand it immediately without having to ask a question about it.

v. Avoid the word "I" and also the word "how" in the final version of your question.

d) The facilitator asks the participants to write down the question in readable letters on a blank card (which he hands out).

e) The instruction is then: walk around the room and find someone. Put the question that is now on your card to the other person. Then ask the other person questions for 3 minutes with the aim of getting them to think about what they are saying. Note: You do not get the opportunity to say something about the question you have formulated. You only ask questions and the other person answers. If the other person says something you do not like, you are not allowed to enter into a discussion. You keep your opinion to yourself. You may only ask short, open questions, not make any other interventions. Also, do not introduce a question like "What I would like to ask is..." You are also not allowed to paraphrase before asking a question. Try to use the other person's words as much as possible in your question.

f) The facilitator does this first with someone! After that, his role is to keep track of time. After 3 minutes, a bell rings and the roles change. If there is no "butterfly" to check on each couple, the facilitator checks that everyone is following the rules.

g) After 2 x 3 minutes the first round is over. The facilitator calls everyone together and asks for their experiences of the first time. Here you can also—depending on what comes along—ask about how the participants ask questions, the types of questions, and so on.

h) Then the participants from the first round exchange the cards. Each participant goes to the second round with the card he just answered. He can still adapt or reformulate the question if he thinks he can make it more general or more interesting.

i) New pairs are formed. The exercise is repeated. The discussion afterwards is also the same.

j) After the second round and the discussion afterwards, the participants exchange cards again and there is again the possibility of adjusting the wording, making it more attractive, and so on.

k) In the third and final round, the participants look for a new partner again and get acquainted briefly. Then, a two-way conversation lasting 3 minutes takes place again. Now, however, there is an additional instruction: after 3 minutes, the person asking the question must be able to repeat the interlocutor's answer to the question and the arguments he has for it in the words of the interlocutor. The facilitator first demonstrates this with a question he reads from someone next to him and with a random participant. Here it is important that the facilitator shows the difference between a reaction to a question and an answer to a question. If the participant does not answer the question, the facilitator must repeat the question until an answer is given.

Example
Question: "What is the added value of having children in a family?" Answer: "Having children indeed brings a lot of changes in the family and so on..." Here, we have not yet answered the question. The questioner may therefore interrupt at the appropriate moment to ask for the answer and the arguments.

l) After the first round, the facilitator selects a few pairs to check whether they have done their work well. This can be discussed in plenary. Afterwards, the roles change with the same exercise.
m) After round three, everyone sits down again for a debriefing. Some questions for the debrief:

   i. What question(s) have stuck in your mind and why?
   ii. What do you think you are learning in this exercise and where?
   iii. What does that teach us about the importance of asking questions in everyday life?

6. The Structure

The musicians are on stage and are silent, concentrating.[17] The moment of the first note has arrived. Ionica breaks the silence and plays an intro that makes many listeners look up. Something special is going to happen here. Everyone is looking at each other. The musicians are watching each other closely. They know who is who and how everyone plays without the need for many words. The guitar player joins in and plays the melodies before the rhythm starts. It is a tacit dialogue, in friendship. It is real contact. The orchestra does not play Romanian music this time, but jazz. The crowd is carried away into something sublime.

How do you start such a concert if you are not as educated as Minune? Who plays the first note? And what happens then? Take a flipchart and a pen. And read on.

6.1. Beforehand: choosing the objectives

In the introduction, you have already read briefly about the results of regular philosophical discussions. They are quite spectacular. And it's not just about the improvement of cognitive abilities. Communication, self-esteem, openness, and empathy are all improved. It is even very beneficial for the wellbeing and the school results of pupils with special (learning) difficulties or a language deficiency. They practice these skills exceptionally well in such a conversation.

To achieve these positive results, one conversation is obviously not enough. You build up something like this with a group slowly. Even with one client/participant there is a lot to be said for starting with exercises in listening, speaking, and arguing, as you found in the previous chapters. After all, many of these competencies come together in a conversation.

At Mimer Elementary School in Norrtälje, Sweden, the pupils are given a philosophy notebook at the start of the school year that lasts for the whole school year.[18] The pupils can take notes, process conversations, draw pictures, and so on. It also contains a list of competencies to be achieved for that school year, for themselves and for the group. Before each exercise or conversation, the pupils (sometimes guided by the teacher) choose what they want to work on. It can be "sitting still" or "listening," "giving an argument" or "assessing an argument." What is chosen depends on the development of the child. The notebook then also serves to evaluate the quality of the conversations.

There is a lot to be said for adopting this Swedish method. As a coach/teacher, you can offer focused exercises which will produce clearer and better results.

For inspiration, there is the score. You can choose aspects of posture or technique that suit your client or target group. A good exercise is to translate these into the language of the client and then let them make their own choice. It is important to formulate the objectives in observable behavior. So, not "The participants respect each other," but "The participants let each other speak."

Below are three examples of checklists. If you are a teacher or teacher trainer, you will like these. After all, they can be filled in more quickly than open-ended questions. But also individual clients like them. You can then evaluate them specifically on the progress of their competencies. You will find an evaluation list for participants, one for facilitators, and one for both. You can have the lists filled in by the participants, by the facilitator, or by the observers/evaluators. All combinations are possible. Please note that they are only meant for inspiration. You still have to do the thinking exercise yourself!

List 1: List for the participants (a group)
(Indicate on a scale of 1=unsatisfactory to 5=very good how well the criterion is fulfilled.)

1. You sit still during the conversation.   O O O O O
2. You are quiet when you are not speaking.   O O O O O
3. You enjoy the research.   O O O O O
4. You say what you want to say as briefly and clearly as possible.   O O O O O
5. You can say why you think what you think.   O O O O O
6. You can give examples.   O O O O O
7. You can specify who answers a question and who does not.   O O O O O
8. You can repeat what you or another person has said.   O O O O O
9. You help another person put into words what he/she says.   O O O O O
10. You put questions to the other participants.   O O O O O

List 2: List for the facilitator
(Rate on a scale of 1 to 10.)

1. The facilitator keeps his/her opinion to himself/herself.
0   10
2. The stimulus used by the facilitator aroused perplexity.
0   10
3. The facilitator suspends his/her judgement as to content.
0   10
4. The facilitator asks the participants what the answer is.
0   10

5. The facilitator asks for arguments.

0   10

6. The facilitator asks the participants to repeat what someone else has said.

0   10

7. The language of the facilitator is adapted to the level of the participants.

0   10

8. The facilitator asks respectively for concreteness and for abstraction when necessary.

0   10

9. The facilitator lets the participants question each other.

0   10

10. The facilitator understands the philosophical problem.

0   10

11. The facilitator was well structured within the time given.

0   10

12. The facilitator listens to the participants.

0   10

List 3: List for both

(Here, rate from "unsatisfactory" to "excellent".)

A. Questions concerning the participants

1. The pupils are encouraged to listen to each other.
Unsatisfactory — Sufficient — Good — Very good — Excellent
2. The pupils enjoy the research.
Unsatisfactory — Sufficient — Good — Very good — Excellent
3. The pupils give answers to the questions.
Unsatisfactory — Sufficient — Good — Very good — Excellent
4. The pupils give arguments and examples.
Unsatisfactory — Sufficient — Good — Very good — Excellent

B. Questions relating to the facilitator

1. The conversation is well introduced.
Unsatisfactory — Sufficient — Good — Very good — Excellent
2. The facilitator does not interfere with the content of the conversation.
Unsatisfactory — Sufficient — Good — Very good — Excellent
3. The facilitator can formulate appropriate instructions.
Unsatisfactory — Sufficient — Good — Very good — Excellent
4. The facilitator critically questions the pupils' reasoning.
Unsatisfactory — Sufficient — Good — Very good — Excellent
5. The facilitator disciplines the pupils' thinking.
Unsatisfactory — Sufficient — Good — Very good — Excellent
6. The facilitator only asks questions.
Unsatisfactory — Sufficient — Good — Very good — Excellent

6.2 The structure of the conversation

Every philosophical conversation in an educational setting (not, for example, spontaneously at home or in a café) has a certain structure. This structure, of course, serves the competencies that are practiced in such a conversation.

The standard structure consists of the elements shown in the diagram.

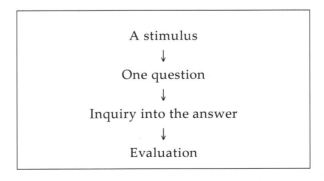

A stimulus
↓
One question
↓
Inquiry into the answer
↓
Evaluation

6.3 The stimulus

The conversation in a class group usually starts with a stimulus. The aim is to offer the participants an experience that creates wonder. Because "wonder" sometimes has confusing, misleading, or romantic connotations, we prefer the term "perplexity."[19] The Plato scholar Gareth Matthews uses this term to explain what might have been the feeling of Socrates' interlocutors, such as Euthyphro. It is the experience of the unexpected, of being shaken up. The participants experience something that they cannot explain, a difficulty or problem where their daily habits of thinking no longer suffice. From this experience, the need arises to ask a question about it.[20]

What can you use as a stimulus to cause this perplexity?

6.3.1. A text fragment

Here you read out a fragment of text or have a participant do so. You choose it or have it chosen in the context of the subject of the lesson. In the bibliography, you will find a few places where you can find useful fragments of text.

6.3.2. An image, photo, or video

Here you stimulate the minds of the participants by showing them something visual.

The instructions you give will, of course, determine how you turn this image into a good research question. The question "What does this image evoke in you?" generates quite different effects than the question "What do you think of this image?" The first question will elicit fewer value-laden responses than the second.

6.3.3. An exercise

You can also offer an activity with a "perplexity" character. Criteria for good exercises are:

- They are relatively simple in terms of instructions and structure.
- They are as short as possible (maximum 10 minutes).
- Preferably they contain concrete, tangible materials (toy animals, photos, and so on).
- They fit in with the living environment of the participants.

Tip for a nice stimulus

a) In pairs, ask the participants to show each other a recent photo they took with their smartphone. Say: "Choose a photo you took recently that you think is remarkable for some reason. You show only that photo (and no other) to your neighbor."

b) Set your alarm bell and say: "Talk about those two pictures for two minutes. After the bell has rung, find one concept that spontaneously came up in your conversation about this."

c) Ask: "In pairs, formulate a question that corresponds to the criteria (see Section 6.4) with a maximum of eight words about this concept (not necessarily about the concept itself)."

6.4. The starting question

You can also start a conversation without a stimulus. In philosophical cafés, for example, it is customary to go straight to a starting question by looking for a question in small groups or choosing one from an existing list.

If there is a stimulus, your task is to formulate a question based on it. You can formulate such a question in small groups or individually. You can ask the participants to formulate a question themselves or choose one from an existing list. The former is preferable because it allows participants to practice formulating such a question. Moreover, it is then about the theme that the group itself finds interesting. If the members of a group are doing this for the first time, they may need some assistance, but after a few times they will get better. The criteria for the question are written on a board or supplied in writing. They are:

- The question is formulated as briefly as possible: maximum ten words.
- The question is open-ended: it does not contain a veiled answer. (An example of a question with a veiled answer is: "Do young people still have a life outside the Internet?" In the word "still," you can hear that the questioner thinks not.)
- There is no right or wrong answer. You must be able to find the answer by thinking about a concept together, not by looking up information. You have to be able to disagree about the answer. So not "Where is the toilet?" but "When do you learn something?"
- Preferably not a "what is" question. This is a question for a definition and invites less research. The question "What is happiness?" means about the same as "When are you happy?", but the latter is more likely to inspire the participant to give examples and arguments from everyday life.
- The question should be immediately understandable: you should not have to ask additional questions (for example, about the stimulus) in order to understand the question.

After the questions have been formulated, collect the questions on the board. If necessary, you go over the questions again to check whether they have all been formulated correctly. However, you do not tinker with the content. Then a question is chosen by a majority. A simple way to do this is to have the participants write down on the board or the flipchart two dashes next to their preferred question and one dash next to their second preferred question. Then add up the dashes.

You can find questions from all philosophical disciplines. Some examples of good starting questions for a philosophical discussion are:

- Are there things without a name? (philosophy of language)
- Does one thing exclude the other? (logic)
- When do you know something for sure? (epistemology)
- When are you allowed to lie? (ethics)
- Is there free will? (ethics/theology)
- When are you independent? (philosophy of education)
- Does God exist? (metaphysics/theology)

In some cases, like the last question, this results in conversations where the link to the experience, or the examples, is hard to find. In a Socratic conversation, the link to the experience is always there. Here are some examples of questions where there is a link to experience:[21]

1. Which question should you not ask?
2. What is a simple question?
3. What can you teach another person?
4. Must you tolerate nonsense?
5. When should you interrupt someone?

6.5. The inquiry

The inquiry is, of course, the core of the concert and should also be the main focus of attention. What the structure looks like depends on the chosen methodology. You will find three types of structure here.

6.5.1. The CoPI meeting

In the early 1970s, Scottish philosopher Catherine McCall appeared at the doors of the Institute for the Advancement of Philosophy for Children (IAPC), founded as a result of the foundational work of Lipman and Sharp. Her assignment was to develop graduate courses for fourth-grade teachers (those who teach children aged 10 and up).[22] It turned out that her group included many teachers of the youngest classes of primary school. The methodology she then developed for philosophizing with young children is presented below. At first glance, it is a fairly simple structure. The participants use a fixed formula every time they say something. This formula includes taking a position, giving arguments, and also showing that they have listened to the other person. The structure of this conversation is shown in the diagram.

The starting question
↓
A first answer from a first-time participant
↓
The answers of the other participants. The formula is
always the same:
↓
"I agree with X when he says Y because Z."
or
"I do not agree with X when he says Y because Z."
↓
Evaluation

In "Y," before giving their arguments, the participants have to repeat verbatim some sentences or part of a sentence from the opinion of one of the previous speakers. This does not have to be the speaker who just came before. It may also be someone who spoke half an hour ago, for example. You can already feel that this obstacle will be frustrating to participants, who will then not be able to say what they think about something. But that's the interesting thing about this method. And this disruption of free speech makes your brain work. Reflection begins where the expression of personal opinion is disrupted. After all, if in a conversation you only repeat what you have thought about something for a long time, you are not reflecting. Here you have to be focused on the other person in order to repeat what they have said. You have to ask yourself whether what you are saying is a contribution to the whole of the conversation. You have to think "in common" and give up your own urge to manifest your thoughts (Po1, Po7). The main task of the facilitator is to guard the structure in which the participants speak.

McCall thought it was important that the children perform this like an orchestra in which she plays the conductor. The facilitator then gives turns to the participants according to his or her own estimation of the depth of the conversation. If the facilitator thinks that Mary could give a good example now, she gives Mary a turn. This would also require philosophical knowledge—to estimate how the conversation could proceed philosophically. This idea is, of course, part of working with the same group for a long time, so that you also know who contributes what at a certain moment. But why not leave the choice of philosophical depth here to the participants themselves? Why should the facilitator at any time have a better estimation of what a person has to contribute than the person himself? This seems to me to be an extra opportunity to practice the technique that is in our score. More specifically, it is about the skill of comparing points of view and arguments and the importance of conceptualization (T2, T8, T14...).

6.5.2. The standard philosophical conversation

The CoPI conversation gives you, as a starting facilitator of philosophical conversations, something to hold on to. You can also use it as an exercise, for example to help the participants learn how to listen to each other. However, soon you may be troubled by the rigidity of the structure. It is not easy to keep this up for long.

The disruptive element in the CoPI methodology lies in the format. A standard philosophical conversation is determined by the way you work through the five movements. The structure of the conversation that you will find below offers some guidance, but there is much more freedom to respond to what happens in the moment itself. Whether that happens will depend on your skills as an "orchestral conductor." First of all, you have to hear what the participants are saying and then ask the right questions. So it is more improvised jazz than score-structured. The structure below is not a plan of how such a conversation would go. It is more like a map to keep in mind. It allows you to mentally reconstruct the different positions and arguments of the participants. You will also recognize the other movements from Chapter 5. Below each movement are some examples of questions you can ask when you have heard this movement and when you want to use it. However, this will be different in every conversation, just like the same piece of improvised jazz music is different in every setting.

So you organize the disagreements first. You harvest subtle and less subtle differences of opinion; the more, the better. This creates the spirit of investigation: what is the situation now, now that we think about something so differently? As time progresses, you can steer the "consensus" as a discussion leader. This does not mean that you strive to reach agreement. Nothing is more suspicious than a philosophical conversation where everyone agrees with each other at the end. What you can do, however, is to determine what the group agrees on and what they do not agree on, and why.

Stimulus

↓

Starting question

↓

First reactions

↓ ↘

To position	**To position**	**To position**
Speaker 1	Speaker 2	Speaker 3
And what do you think?	*What about it?*	*Do you agree with X?*

↓ ↘

To argue	**To argue**	**To argue**
Speaker 1	Speaker 2	Speaker 3
Why is this so?	*How so?*	*Why are you saying this now?*
How so?	*Why?*	*Why do you call it that?*

↘

To abstract

Yes, and?
What does this have to do with the question?
What do you call this?
What is this example/your story about?

↘

To concretize

Where did this happen?
Who did what? Who said what? How did it happen? What does it mean here?
What is that about?
Have you experienced this?
Do you have an example of this?

↓ ↘

To listen
Speaker 1
What did X just say?

To listen
Speaker 2
*Who can say
that again?*

To listen
Speaker 3
*How did he/she say
that?*

↓ ↘

To investigate
Speaker 1   Speaker 2   Speaker 3

What do you think about what you said?
What does that have to do with the question?
Which reason is the most important?
Why?
What do you think of how you are reasoning now?
Does X now agree with Y?
What reasons has X given for what he/she thinks? Why does he/she think so? And what do you think about this yourself?
Do we now have an answer to our question?
What do we agree on so far? What do we not agree on?
What progress have we made in the conversation?
Where have we gone?

The structure of the conversation is shown in the next diagram.

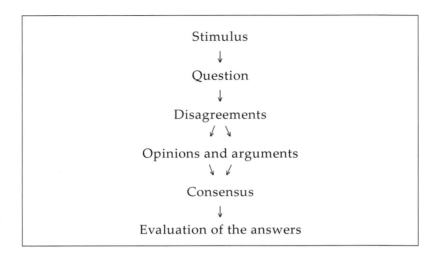

Stimulus
↓
Question
↓
Disagreements
↙ ↘
Opinions and arguments
↘ ↙
Consensus
↓
Evaluation of the answers

6.5.3. The Socratic conversation

In the previous two forms of structure, you work with a stimulus that leads to a question and that preferably comes from the group. The stimulus is the reason for formulating the question. There is no further reference to it in the subsequent conversation. In the Socratic conversation (from the Nelsonian tradition) the facilitator does not offer a stimulus. The participants themselves undergo a joint experience or tell about an experience that then functions as research material for the question throughout the conversation. What is typical, then, is this focus on the experience. A Socratic conversation is, in one sentence, a research conversation in which a group or a pair of people investigate the truth of the opinions they have about their experience.[23]

So, in the structure of a "classic" Socratic conversation, you focus on one experience in which one participant does or says or has done something and about which he makes a claim in terms of the question. In the story of that experience you then focus on one moment about which that assertion is made. For example, if the question is "What is a simple question?", you might first ask a participant if they have had a recent experience of hearing or asking a simple question. The accompanying statement should also be about a specific moment in that experience. It should be phrased in terms of the question. A good formulation is: "When X did Y, that was Z (the words from the question)." For example, someone's statement in a conversation might be: "When Mum asked me at dinner yesterday 'Do you want salt on your potatoes?' that was a simple question." When you have the assertion, ask the narrator the arguments he has for this assertion. Here, for example, it might be: "because there are only seven words in the question."

So the first thing you do as a facilitator is to ask for the moment in the experience, the corresponding claim, and the arguments of one participant, and write down the words of the narrator without interfering with the content. In the case of a group discussion, you then ask the group: "What do you think of this?" Then the investigation begins: Is this question indeed a simple one at that moment? And why? The trick here is to continue asking for the arguments so that the group discusses the reasons for calling this question simple in the first place. Is the number of words a good or sufficient reason here? Are there other, better reasons? Or is it not a simple question at all? What then comes up for discussion are the ideas that the participants have in their heads about "simplicity," but this is done indirectly. After all, you are not looking for a definition; rather, you are investigating the spontaneous interpretation of an experience. It is about whether you can rightly or wrongly call Mama's question about the potatoes simple. The same goes for other concepts like freedom, justice, and so on.

The structure is shown in the diagram.

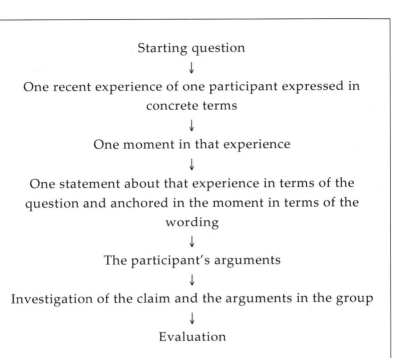

There are different ways to start such a conversation. You can formulate a question yourself as a facilitator, or you can let participants choose from a few questions based on their experiences with such a question. Or you let the participants tell you about a recent experience and then look for a pithy moment in it and formulate the question afterwards. The first form is the easiest. Leading such a conversation is not a trick; it is a real craft.[24] Especially in the research phase, a lot of things happen that cannot be predicted. An experienced facilitator will be able to hold the line by using the five verbs from the score as a guide: positioning, arguing, listening, concretizing/abstracting, and researching. The Socratic dialogue is an art in itself. After all, there is no group to do the critical questioning and the discussion leader leads it himself.[25]

So, leading a Socratic conversation requires training. But don't let that discourage you. Give it a try. Below is an exercise in which the structure provides sufficient support. This time it is about an experience in the here and now, not a story from the past. The big advantage is that the involvement of each participant is immediately much greater. Moreover, it is not necessary to write out such a story; everyone has seen and experienced it and can refer to it. If you want to try it the classical way, with a story from the past, the step-by-step plan and the article in the endnote will start you off.[26]

Exercise: Short Socratic conversation about a here-and-now experience

Objectives and target group
This exercise is suitable for a group of six to twelve participants, aged 10 and up.

The objectives that are practiced are:

Po2 + 3 + 6–11; T6–23; Pe1–22

Time and supplies
This exercise takes 60 minutes. You will need a large room, chairs arranged in a circle, a flipchart with sheets, one notepad or notebook per person. You will also need as many markers and pens as there are participants. And you will need a box of toy blocks. The word "you" here means "the facilitator."

Activity
This is a Socratic conversation without a starting question. It starts with an experience and the inquiry is about the understanding of the experience.

1. The start

You explain the structure of the exercise: first, a here-and-now experience with the blocks, then you will ask the participants for an opinion about what happened there, and then they will have a Socratic discussion about one of those opinions until the time is up.

2. The experience (15 minutes)

You give each participant a handful of blocks. Make sure that everyone has about the same number in their hand. Then you give the assignment. Write the assignment on the flipchart. The assignment reads:

Make a tower together as high as possible with the blocks. You have to use all the blocks. No block may remain on the table. You may make the tower a maximum of two times.

The group is given 15 minutes. You set an alarm clock. When the alarm bell rings, everyone drops all the blocks, no matter where they are in the exercise.

While the participants are at it, cut the flipchart sheets in half and place a stack in the middle of the circle.

3. The claims and the arguments (10 minutes)

You do not comment on the exercise or rate it.

You give each participant a sheet of paper from a notepad, a pen, half a sheet of paper from the flipchart, and a marker.

You say:

> *Find one moment during this exercise that you found remarkable. Write this down on the sheet of paper in one sentence in very concrete terms. For example: "Marc took the cube from Karen to start the next floor." Then take the flipchart and write your opinion on it with a marker. Use the following formula: "When X did/said Y, it was Z because..." And after the "because," write the reasons why you think that what he shows there is what you think. Example: "When Marc took the block from Karen, I thought that was brave because Karen did not dare to put it down herself."*

Ask them to write their first names at the bottom of the flipchart sheet.

4. Study the flipchart sheets and choose a topic (7 minutes)

You hang the flipchart sheets next to each other. Then you read them all. You ask if anything is not clear. If something is not clear to someone, you ask the author to explain it and then you correct what is on the sheet. This is purely a matter of clarification. If a participant starts to criticize one of the sheets, ask them to wait a little longer.

When everything is clear, ask: "Which one stands out to you because you really agree with it or disagree with it?" Let the participants think about this for a few minutes. Then you give each of them the opportunity to speak briefly. You do not start a discussion yet. Afterwards, you pick out one opinion based on the one that has the most energy and attention of the group. You propose to the group: "Do you mind if we talk about idea X?" Suppose there is not that much energy; in that case, after the round you ask the participants to put a total of three spheres on the flipchart sheets with their markers: two spheres on the sheet with the opinion they find most interesting, and one sphere on the sheet with their second choice. The discussion continues using the sheet that has collected the most spheres.

5.   Gather other views on that single moment (7 minutes)

You now ask each of the participants to come and sit in the circle and to write on the notepad or the notebook what they think about this. Ask them to do this in the same structure as the one on the sheet. If they agree with the statement, ask them why. If they disagree, likewise.

So for example: *"When Marc took the cube from Karen, it wasn't courageous—he was just impatient."*

When everyone has written down their response, ask them to compare it with what their neighbor has written down and talk about it.

6. Interview (10 minutes)

You now tell the participants that we are going to do some research until the alarm clock stops. You set the alarm clock to a certain length of time, depending on the time available. A minimum is 10 minutes; there is no maximum. You now ask the participants: "Who has read something interesting in their neighbor's house?" You wait for someone to take the lead. You let the group discuss this. You do not intervene with regard to the content; you just ask questions.

What you do as a facilitator in the conversation is:

- You make sure that the focus remains on the chosen sheet of flipchart paper. For example, if someone says: *"We didn't work well together,"* you ask: *"What does this have to do with Marc being brave?"* If someone brings in an experience, for example *"I found it irritating to have to do this under time pressure,"* you ask, *"What does this mean for that moment when Marc took the block?"*
- You look for differences of opinion and arguments: *"Has Marc been courageous or not, and why?"* (positioning + arguing)
- You ask what someone says about the moment Marc grabbed the block: *"Where did you see that?"* (concretizing)
- You ask participants to repeat what someone else has said: *"Can you repeat what Anke just said?"* (listening)
- You ask for arguments in favor of the arguments, e.g. *"Why do you think taking the initiative is not the same as being brave?"* (exploring)

7. Conclusion (10 minutes)

When the bell has rung, ask the participants to write down for themselves in the notebook what they now think of the chosen position. Ask them to use the following formula:

"It's true that Marc was brave then because..."
or
"It's not true that Marc was brave then because..."

You ask a few people who want to share that in the group. The group does not discuss it any further. Everyone just reads out his or her sentence.

You conclude with one or more of the following questions:

- "What have we agreed on and what are we not yet agreed on?"
- "What did you think of this conversation?"
- "What did you practice during this conversation?"
- "What have you learned about X (e.g. 'being brave')?"

In the follow-up discussion, as a facilitator, pay attention to the following :

- When someone asks a question about the course of the conversation, ask whether there are others who have also chosen this moment. Then ask what they thought of it.
- Nobody is obliged to share anything; just make sure that those who want to say something can.

- If someone continues with the content, ask: "Can you say something about an intervention in the conversation that struck you?"
- Question views again Socratically where appropriate. If, for example, someone says: "*I thought it was going a bit slowly,*" you can ask them to be more specific: "*Where exactly did you think it was going slowly? What do you think is the cause of that? How do others see it?*"
- Make sure that you do not "defend" yourself as a facilitator. Keep it to why something was noticed.
- If you work with an evaluation list of objectives, you can use this for the follow-up discussion. You can then ask, for example, what participants have learned from this conversation.

Variants

You can expand this exercise by offering different activities. You can also work with a large group in, say, three rounds of discussions. In the first round, an inner circle of ten conducts the conversation for 10 minutes; the outer circle observes. Then the roles are reversed, and in the third round you work in plenary. The discussion afterwards can also be more extensive, depending on the time available and the objectives.

If you are working with a group of observers, their task depends on the focus of your objectives. You should preferably give them a few questions to work with before the evaluation.

You can also keep it to one task:

Find one participant's intervention that struck you, and note how the others and the facilitator dealt with it. Why did you notice it? What question do you have about it?

Furthermore, the observers are instructed to remain silent. If they want to intervene, they are not allowed to.

You have the observers write down their response in their notebook. During the discussion afterwards, they can exchange it, for instance in pairs, and then in plenary if time permits.

6.6. The evaluation

In principle, a philosophical conversation ends when time is up. If it is good, it is left open because no answer to the question has been found or a consensus has not been reached. You may find better answers than at the beginning of the conversation but never *the* answer.

However, you can close a few minutes before the end in a certain way. You can evaluate either the content or the form/competencies.

If you want to evaluate the **content**, here are some possible guiding questions:

- What idea that was new to you did you hear in this conversation?
- Is your answer different now than it was at the beginning?
- If someone were to ask you the starting question in the street today, what would you answer?
- Who do you think said something interesting?

- What did we agree on and why, and what did we disagree on and why?
- What do you think needs to be investigated further?

You can also end the session artistically, for example by inviting the participants to draw, model, or represent the answer to the question.

If you want to evaluate the **form**, you can ask participants to refer again to the philosophical notebook or the list of competencies. You can discuss this individually, in pairs or triplets, and/or in plenary. Ideally, in a group discussion, it should be done in that order. This way, everyone has the opportunity to evaluate his/her progress in the competencies first. Then you can check with the others whether they recognize this. Then you can evaluate the conversation in general in a plenary session.

7. The Goal

In an interview, Ionica talks about playing together and befriending Toni Iordache.[27] They could apparently play together for hours and only pause to drink an occasional glass of wine. From this you can see that for Ionica playing music is about pleasure and friendship, but it is also simply a passion. He can play for 24 hours in a row, he says, because he cannot do otherwise. It is the love of music—it has its own meaning.

Is it the same with philosophical conversations? Are you essentially doing it for fun? Yes, actually. There are people who like it very much and there are people who don't like it at all. But it's not just fun for fun's sake. If you, as a non-expert, listen to Ionica, you might find the music nervously plucked. If you, as a non-expert, observe a philosophical conversation, you might also find it crazy. You might find it to be "making a mountain out of a molehill" or "making unnecessary difficulties." If you listen more closely, however, you will see that there is a reason why the musicians enter into this complexity and interact so beautifully. It is not just out of friendship. Precisely through all that complexity, they want to create harmony, beauty. That is why participants in a philosophical conversation go on so much about their differences of opinion. They want to know exactly how things are. They want to hear all the details and all the difficulties because they are looking for more truth.

That sort of precision of meaning is not so popular these days. You may think that "the truth does not exist." If you really think that, you will have to convince the other person of the truth of what you think. And if you think that convincing is not important, that you can just be silent about it, then why is that true?

This last chapter will test your nerves to the full. It starts with a conversation between philosophers about truth. The start is a bit more scholarly and academic than that of the previous two conversations: a text by Friedrich Nietzsche, the philosopher who like no other puts his readers on their mettle.

7.1. The prejudices of the philosophers

A group of P4C facilitators are gathered for a philosophical discussion. Their names are Mark, Charles, Nicole, and her friend Yvonne. Anny is also there. She has only recently started as a facilitator. She has also brought along her husband Tony.

They start with a stimulus: a text by Nietzsche, the first paragraph of the first chapter of *Beyond Good and Evil*, entitled 'On the Prejudices of Philosophers.' The participants read the text in silence. And then the following conversation takes place.[28]

Extract from the first chapter of *Beyond Good and Evil*
On the Prejudices of the Philosophers

Friedrich Nietzsche

The will to truth which will still tempt us to many a venture, that famous truthfulness of which all philosophers so far have spoken with respect—what questions has this will to truth not laid before us! What strange, wicked, questionable questions! That is a long story even now—and yet it seems as if it had scarcely begun. Is it any wonder that we should finally become suspicious, lose patience, and turn away impatiently? that we should finally learn from this Sphinx to ask questions, too? Who is it really that puts questions to us here? What in us really wants "truth"? Indeed we came to a long halt at the question about the cause of this will—until we finally came to a complete stop before a still more basic question. We asked about the value of this will. Suppose we want truth: why not rather untruth? and uncertainty? even ignorance?

The problem of the value of truth came before us—or was it we who came before the problem? Who of us is Oedipus here? Who the Sphinx? It is a rendezvous, it seems, of questions and question marks.

And though it scarcely seems credible, it finally almost seems to us as if the problem had never even been put so far—as if we were the first to see it, fix it with our eyes, and risk it. For it does involve a risk, and perhaps there is none that is greater.

Facilitator (F): Is there anyone who has any thoughts on this text?

Anny: Yes, I think it's a bit of a heavy text.

F: Why?

Anny: About the truth and so on. I immediately get tired of that. There is no such thing as the truth, is there? Everyone has their own truth!

Tony: Nietzsche was a fool, wasn't he, Anny? Wasn't he a syphilis patient? Someone who writes texts like this is sick in the head, if you ask me!

(There is a chuckle.)

Mark: But it's not about the truth at all. That's not in the text.

Well, that's opened it up—and how! To use a Nietzschean image: the lion roars! The text functions as Nietzsche would have wanted: like a fox in a henhouse. The first three hens immediately have a very different reaction. Anny doesn't really say anything about the text. She says something about her own perception of it, asks a rhetorical question, and throws a one-liner into the group. We don't have a position here yet. We do have one with Tony. But he raves about supposed personal characteristics of Nietzsche. It doesn't look as if he's willing to engage with this text. He just babbles. Mark has a completely different attitude. What he notices is that something is said about something that is not in the text. This intervention is rewarded. The facilitator responds to it.

F: So what is it about, Mark?

Mark: Nietzsche talks about the will to truth and why we want truth. I think that is a good question. What in us actually wants truth?

F: And what is your answer to that question, Mark?

Mark: I don't know; I'll have to think about that.

Charles: I think that it's to do with survival. We want truth because otherwise we are misled and our chances of survival diminish.

F: So what is your short answer to Nietzsche's question, Charles? What is it in us that seeks truth then?

Charles: Well, our survival instinct.

Tony: (Shrilly.) Survive—come on! If I'm going to survive this bullshit here, it's going to have to be good!

F: Anny, do you meanwhile agree with Mark that it is not about the truth in the text?

Anny: Yes, "the" truth. That's not in there, that's right.

F: So is it true what Mark said when he said, "That's not in the text"?

Anny: Yes.

While her husband Tony is still ranting, Anny is more committed. Or at least she is tempted to make a statement that is "true": that it is not in the text. In doing so, she adopts the same attitude as Mark and Charles: she is in the study, she is interested (P06). But now the facilitator presses her to explain how her statement that something is true is consistent with her earlier view that "everyone has their own truth." The facilitator will not let that go. He goes at it like a pitbull.

F: Anny, you said earlier that everyone has their own truth. Is what you say, then, "your own truth" or is it just true?

Anny: I don't understand that.

F: You just said "Everyone has their own truth," is that right?

Anny: Yes, I think so, yes.

F: So if you say, "It is true what Mark says that the truth is not in the text," is that Mark's own truth? That means that you also have your own truth, and what is that?

Anny: (Thinks.) No, I said he is right that it is not in the text. I meant to say that everyone has a different opinion. "'The truth' in itself does not exist."

F: OK, so you're saying that "Everyone has a different opinion" is more true than "Everyone has their own truth"?

A: Yes, that is more accurate, yes.

F: And is it therefore more true?

(Tony attracts attention by pressing his index finger to his head and making an "Oh my god" face. He looks at everyone.)

Anny: (Thinks.) Yes, I don't know if that's true anymore. I don't know yet if everyone here in the group has a different opinion; I've only heard a few. But I suppose so, yes.

F: And if we ask for it and it turns out to be true, would it be true what you said?

Anny: In that case, yes.

The facilitator helps Anny here by nuancing her earlier opinion that "everyone has their own truth" into "everyone has a different opinion." That seems like nitpicking and many people would say that in an everyday conversation. They would think it merely a semantic issue. Why is this accuracy in language important? It has to do with a classic way of thinking about truth: you look for the similarity between what is said in language and what is the case in reality. So every word refers to something else unless it is a synonym of another word. That is why the facilitator also asks here for the distinction between "right" and "true." "Correctly stated" is not the same thing as "more the case." The latter, says Anny, is something she does not know yet. While Anny is being philosophically cultivated here, Tony is still being ignored. Meanwhile, Charles's position on the survival instinct has not yet been tested against this idea of the truth. That is still on the table. The facilitator knows this and asks about it.

F: OK, Charles, have you seen anything of a survival instinct in the behavior of Anny during this discussion?

Charles: No, but she didn't really want to find the truth either.

F: Why?

Charles: No, you have seduced her into another point of view. Nietzsche speaks of something in us that wants truth. I saw that more in you than in her.

F: How come?

Nicole: (Intervening.) Yes, that's right. (Turns to facilitator.) You wanted her to abandon her view that "everyone has their own truth," which she eventually did.

(Yvonne nods.)

F: Do you see in me a will to truth, then?

Nicole: Yes, you are aiming at that in any case. You think it's not true that everyone has their own truth, and you want her to see that.

F: Is it true? Is it true that what Nicole is saying is what I want to make you see?

Yvonne: Yes, I noticed that too. I think so too.

The facilitator did not expect this. He suddenly comes under fire himself. He asked for the reference for the "we" that wants truth because of the survival instinct. Is there anyone in this group who qualifies for this? Anny? No, according to Charles, Nicole and, tacitly, Yvonne too. The one who comes closest is the facilitator himself. He is aiming at something. But the question "What is there in us that wants truth?" has not yet been answered with the facilitator as a reference. We only have Nicole's statement that the facilitator wanted Anny "to see something." Therefore, he asks about this again.

F: So, to repeat Nietzsche's question, "what in me" is it that wants that?

Nicole: I would say power. You want her to see something; you want to be right.

F: And what is the difference with Charles's point of view?

Nicole: What was that then?

F: Who can articulate the difference between Nicole's point of view and Charles's?

Mark: They both talk about your intervention in which they saw that will to truth that Nietzsche talked about. And

Charles thought that what that is in you is probably survival instinct. And Nicole calls it power.

The reason why the facilitator here asks for the difference between Nicole's and Charles's point of view to be brought into focus again has to do with truth. They are both about what the facilitator does. But if other names are used for this, such as "survival instinct" and "power," then there is also work to be done. Then we have to agree on what to call it. Truth is sought here by seeking agreement on what to call something. To explore this further, the facilitator opens it up to Mark. But Mark provides a whole new perspective!

F: And what do you think, Mark?

Mark: I don't know if you or anyone else here in the group would want truth. Maybe you do; maybe you don't. But Nietzsche doesn't talk about that either.

F: Why?

Mark: No, he puts "truth" inside quotation marks in his text! His question is: What in us actually wants "truth"? I don't think that is a coincidence. He has done it deliberately.

Anny: (Enthusiastically.) Yes, yes, that's true. It's in quotation marks!

Tony: Great, Anny! You're already becoming as mad as Nietzsche himself. But he was a nitpicker because he had nothing else to fuck, wasn't he! (Laughs loudly and looks around.)

F: (Not moving a muscle, not making eye contact with Tony, looking at Mark.) And what do you think the fact that it's in quotation marks means, Mark?

Mark: That "truth" does not actually exist and is therefore a word that does not make sense. And that perhaps we are looking for something that does not exist.

F: Is that what Mark says?

Charles: Yes, that's right. In the question in the text, it says "truth" in quotation marks. But I don't know what that means.

F: So is what Mark said true or "true" in quotation marks? (All laugh except Tony.)

7.2. Seeking truth or being right?

In the Middle Ages, Thomas Aquinas and others of the time called the criterion of truth "the correspondence of the thing and the intellect" (*adaequatio rei et intellectus*). In tradition, this was called the "correspondence theory." The statement "This is a chair" is true if it corresponds to the actual chair. Mark's statement "That is not in the text" claims truth from this theory. Of course, this distinction caused a lot of problems in philosophy, for how can we know what facts are separate from our thought processes? One of the problems is that while you can speak of an isolated statement and its relation to reality, a statement is always connected to other statements. The "coherence theory" is therefore a complement to the correspondence theory. It says that you have to look at that relation between statement and reality in the total system of statements in which it is found to be true. There must be coherence between what you as an individual say about that chair and what other interlocutors say about it. In other words, as long as someone holds a different belief about the same facts, there is work to be done. Then we have to argue further until we agree on what we see in reality. So what we do in a philosophical conversation is this. It is increasing the intersubjective truth. It happens here, for example, when Nicole's finding that what truth wants in us is "power" is compared with Charles's finding that it is rather "survival instinct."

There is more than the intersubjective assessment in a conversation. Speaking the truth happens between people and they may or may not be convinced by such a statement. For example, if Nicole says that the facilitator wants power in the conversation, this is more convincing if it is accompanied by an argument or an observation that is so powerful that it convinces everyone, so that, in other words, she is right. She did not do that. Mark did have that convincing power when he pointed out that what Anny was talking about, the truth, was not in the text, but the "will to truth" was. That remark was consensually true and for that reason influential for this truth-seeking audience.

But being right is not enough. A message is only convincing if, in addition to the *logos* (the rational content of the message), the *pathos* (the ability to touch the feelings of the audience with the message) and the *ethos* (the person of the speaker as expressed by his will or intention) are also taken care of. Ethos is the speaker's virtue as expressed in his reasoning, his righteousness, and his benevolence towards his interlocutor. If the interlocutor feels a match on that level, he will be open to the message; otherwise not. In other words, in a philosophical conversation, participants must want the same thing—that conversation. Anny is attracted to this will, but her husband Tony is not. He is not attuned to the others and, for that reason, no one responds to what he says. If there is no investigation, any truth-telling will be ineffective. Finally, a match is also needed at the level of feelings. Only if your words and arguments are impressive, and touch on what the interlocutor is sensitive to, will they be heard and the interlocutor be open to the new perspective. That is why Mark gets Anny excited and Tony gets nobody excited.

7.3. What shall we do with the drunken Tony?

There is something much more serious going on with Tony than just a communication mismatch. He seems to think the whole enterprise is a waste of time, but makes no effort to explain why. Despite this intellectual laziness, he does demand a lot of attention. His position is that of the troublemaker. What he shows is an indifference to the truth. He interprets everything in his own terms and wants to ridicule the whole enterprise. He overrides the others and, among other things, insults his wife in front of everyone. Tony here represents a type of participant that you come across more often in the so-called "post-truth" era. They have no judgement in the sense of a thoughtful opinion. They have not thought about anything, but they do demand attention. They are not stupid. They just set themselves above the truth-seekers and cheat; they want to divert attention or deliberately mislead people to their advantage.

How does the facilitator deal with this? He ignores Tony. There are good reasons for doing so here. In an individual consultation, of course, that is not possible; in that case you can work on the attitude and the technique to make a better philosopher out of your zealot. In a group, it's different. Such a disruptive person feeds on a group that is still searching for truth. Not only this; he/she also makes it more difficult for the group to work together. This ties in with an entirely different theory of truth: pragmatism. The pragmatists had a different argument than the correspondence or coherence thinkers. For them truth is also practical. After all, you have to survive and also live and work together. The motivation for getting it right or seeking agreement with each other is not love of truth — you just want to be able to function well. That includes being as efficient as possible with each other and with things. That is why you also rely on other truth-seekers. If you make an appointment with the doctor and she says, "I can come at 5 p.m.," you assume that she is not lying. That is more practical for both parties. If it turns out that the doctor was joking, cheating, and therefore making fun of you, the only effect is that she gets a lot of attention and you get scared because she can't be trusted. It is therefore more practical to tell the truth. Truth is what works. But are we talking about the truth or the "truth" in quotation marks as in Nietzsche's text?

7.4. Become a fool?

If Nietzsche is right that in a philosophical conversation we pursue something that is "in quotation marks," the whole enterprise has at once a tragic but also an ironic and funny, light character. According to him, the *Übermensch* was someone who had thoroughly understood perspectivism in everything and who therefore came to the conclusion that we wander in darkness in search of light. What does this mean for participants in philosophical conversations? It means that in addition to the serious competencies you could read in the score, something more fundamental is practiced. The confrontation with perspectives that are entirely different from your own compels you to contemplate this spectacle. It is an invitation to play and contemplate simultaneously the game of truth. Contemplation is accompanied by a sense of joy and freedom. It is a liberated, broad-minded soul that at the same time throws itself passionately onto the battlefield in search of the truth and examines it in order to be able to put it into perspective. This is also the secret of enjoyment. You go for it and you can let go at the same time. It is a passionate distance (Po11).

If you're trained in thinking, speaking, and listening, you become not only a master in conversation but also a "fool" like Socrates. You become liberated from limited perspectives. You do not remain on lonely heights like Buddha but, like the later Buddha, you find yourself in the middle of society, in the middle of everyday conversation. This time, however, you're transformed into someone who plays, who enjoys, and lets others enjoy. A philosophically developed "self" has a naive egoism in which, because it is so light and good, it is also immediately good and light for others. It does not try to be like that. It is so. It is a good citizen of its own accord. And it inspires others in that way.

In doing so, you do not give up the traditional thrust of the philosophical conversation—the search for which statements are true and which are false. You do not go as far as to claim that you are not ultimately concerned with truth, but with finding meaning or spirituality or the art of living or better relations with others. Nor do you claim that everything is just a game. You don't want to end your last concert on a false note, do you? No, you want a beautiful and surprising final chord! So if, on your deathbed, you claim that you have always had philosophical conversations in order to become as light as a feather in life, then you will die satisfied. You have become as light as a feather in life partly because of these conversations. But also because this last statement, namely that "becoming as light as a feather" was the ultimate goal of your philosophical conversations, is simply true.

Notes

1   https://www.youtube.com/watch?v= EO0eRrdsPpk. Search term: 'Orchestra "Lautarii" si Maestrul Nicolae Botgros din concertul "Dorul Basarabiei."' At the beginning of each chapter, you will find a link to a YouTube fragment about Minune, always in an endnote. All these excerpts are accompanied by a QR code that allows you to listen to the piece of music directly on your smartphone.

2   There have been many empirical studies on the effects of philosophical conversations, especially at school. Prof. Dr. Griet Galle (KU Leuven) made an overview (in Dutch) of recent reliable studies in 2020. See Galle, G. (2019), Waarom en hoe filosoferen in de klas, *School en klaspraktijk*, 61 (1), pp. 27–33; and Galle, G. (2020), De effecten van filosoferen met kinderen in de klas, *School en klaspraktijk*, 61 (3), pp. 37–45.

3   See https://www.youtube.com/watch?v=h2lgvQxShLE. Search term: 'Hora de la nord orchestra Lautarii.'

4   https://youtu.be/GCTd4n97NJI. Search term: 'Ionica Minune. La nunta Lui Marius Turneanu.'

5   https://www.youtube.com/watch?v=kGLibQLwqvg. Search term: 'Ionica Minune. Revelionul Muzicantilor (Lautarilor) Craiova 2019.'

6   The Belgian philosopher Luce Irigaray wrote beautifully about this "silence presque absolue" in her book on the impossibility of grasping love through language. See Irigaray, L. (1992), *J'aime à toi*, Paris: Grasset, pp. 179–186.

7   The French philosopher Frédéric Lenoir believed that students should be trained not only in critical thinking but also in attentiveness. He founded the 'Sève Foundation,' which today operates in French-speaking Belgium, Canada, France, Switzerland, and elsewhere. In accordance

with the founder's idea, the facilitators working for this foundation always start the philosophical conversation with a meditation exercise. See www.sevebelgium.org.

8   The Plato translation used here is from Hamilton, E. and Cairns, H. (eds.) (1961), *The collected dialogues of Plato*, Princeton: Princeton University Press.

9   https://www.youtube.com/ watch?v=dZa3bv288A8. Search term: 'Ionica Minune M-as duce pe o carare si Urca oile la munte.'

10 A nice introduction to critical thinking is the work of Stella Cottrell. See e.g. Cottrell, S. (2023), *Critical thinking skills: Effective analysis, argument and reflection*, Second Edition, Palgrave Macmillan.

11 https://www.youtube.com/ watch?v=v_y88zd7Ano. Search term: 'Kaliakra & Ionica Minune jam on Romanian TV.'

12 It was a kind of cadet school for international socialism, in which the members were often harshly trained in "character and independent spirit": no alcohol, only vegetarian food, lots of sports...and thus also philosophical conversations. The Walkemühle no longer exists. But the Philosophical-Political Academy, founded by Nelson, still does. The school survived the Second World War and still organizes Socratic discussions in the Nelsonian style. It is worth taking part in. Together with a group of enthusiasts ranging in age from 18 to 88, you take an entire weekend to answer one question. And this is done rigorously, step by step, with a firm discipline reminiscent of the regime in the Walkemühle. See http://www.philosophisch-politische-akademie.de.

13 He called it "Socratically guided exercises." For a nice overview see Boers, E. (2022), *From science to conscience: The Socratic dialogue reconsidered*, Enschede: Gildeprint.

14 He makes a strict distinction between "dogmatic" and "Socratic" teachers. Dogmatic teachers are those who

have a judgement with the intention of teaching someone something. By introducing this distinction, of course, he himself gets into trouble if he wants to be a Socratic teacher himself. See Nelson, L. (1922), The Socratic method, reprinted in Saran, R. & Neisser, B. (2004), *Enquiring minds*, Trentham: Trentham Books.

15 For a detailed discussion of the importance of this democratic character, see Echeverria, E. & Hannam, P. (2017), The community of philosophical inquiry (P4C): A pedagogical proposal for advancing democracy, in Rollins Gregory, M., Haynes, J., & Murris, K. (eds.), *The Routledge international handbook of philosophy for children* (pp. 3–10), London and New York: Routledge.

16 McCall, C.C. (2009), *Transforming thinking: Philosophical inquiry in the primary and the secondary classroom*, London: Routledge.

17 https://www.youtube.com/watch?v=fgD2MTTtPh8. Search term: 'Ionica Minune Franta 2015.'

18 The results of this approach in Mimer were used in Ann Pihlgren's PhD. See Pihlgren, A. (2008), *Socrates in the classroom: Rationales and effects of philosophizing with children*, Stockholm: Stockholm University Press.

19 For more on wonder, see 'The Art of Wonder: Interview with Kristof Van Rossem,' *Okra magazine*, December 2018; available for download at www.socraticdialogue.be.

20 Matthews, G. (2002), *Socratic perplexity and the nature of philosophy*, Oxford: Oxford University Press.

21 My colleague Hans Bolten collected a lot of starting questions for a Socratic conversation that you can find at www.socratischgesprek.nl under 'materials.'

22 McCall, C.C. *(2009), Transforming thinking: Philosophical inquiry in the primary and the secondary classroom*, London: Routledge.

23 More about the Socratic conversation can be found at www.socratischgesprek.be. See also further Bolten, H. & Van Rossem, K. (2014), Socratisch beraad, in Van Dartel, H. & Molewijk, B. (eds.), *In gesprek blijven over goede zorg* (pp. 96–112), Amsterdam: Boom.

24 For a nice illustration of how such a conversation proceeds and what the facilitator then does, see Van Rossem, K. (2018), How to lead a Socratic dialogue, in Staude, D. & Ruschmann, E. (eds.), *Understanding the other and oneself* (pp. 67–80), Cambridge: Cambridge Scholars.

25 For more on this, see Van Rossem, K. (2012), Het socratisch tweegesprek, *Filosofie en Praktijk* 33 (3), pp. 123–129.

26 That roadmap can be found, along with other roadmaps, in Bolten, H. & Van Rossem, K. (2014), Socratisch beraad, in Van Dartel, H. & Molewijk, B. (eds.), *In gesprek blijven over goede zorg* (pp. 96–112), Amsterdam: Boom. Here you will also find more explanation of the five movements. If you would like more training in facilitating Socratic conversations, you can find more information at www. socratischgesprek.be.

27 https://www.youtube.com/watch?v=0kRuw8p-V90. Search term: 'Ionica Minune interview.'

28 Nietzsche, F. (2002), *Beyond good and evil*, Cambridge: CUP.

Bibliography

1. Read more about philosophical conversation

Brenifier, O. (2004). *La pratique de la philosophie à l'école primaire: Manuel pour les enseignants du primaire et du collège.* Paris: Sedrap.

Brenifier, O. (2018). *The art of philosophical practice.* Available through http://www.pratiques-philosophiques.fr/wp-content/uploads/2018/04/artofpp-1.pdf

Galle, G. (2019). Waarom en hoe filosoferen in de klas. *School en klaspraktijk,* 61 (1), pp. 27–33.

Galle, G. (2020). De effecten van filosoferen met kinderen in de klas. *School en klaspraktijk,* 61 (3), pp. 37–45.

Haynes, J. (2002). *Children as philosophers.* London: Routledge.

Kienstra, N. (2016). *Effective philosophizing in the classroom: Getting teachers to create their own lesson designs in the school subject of philosophy.* Enschede: Ipskamp.

Lipman, M. (1988). *Philosophy goes to school.* Philadelphia: Temple University.

Lipman, M. (1991). *Thinking in education.* Cambridge: Cambridge University Press.

Martens, E. (2000). *Spelen met denken: Over filosoferen met kinderen.* Rotterdam: Lemniscaat.

McCall, C.C. (2009). *Transforming thinking: Philosophical inquiry in the primary and the secondary classroom.* London: Routledge.

Pihlgren, A. (2008). *Socrates in the classroom: Rationales and effects of philosophizing with children.* Stockholm: Stockholm University Press.

Rollins Gregory, M., Haynes, J., & Murris, K. (2017). *The Routledge international handbook of philosophy for children.* London and New York: Routledge.

Rondhuis, N.T.W. (2005). *Philosophical talent: Empirical investigations into philosophical features of adolescents' discourse.* Rotterdam: Veenman.

Schleifer, M. & Poirier, G. (1995). The effect of philosophical discussions in the classroom on respect for others and non-stereotypic attitudes. *Thinking: The Journal of Philosophy for Children*, 12 (4), pp. 32–34.

Splitter, L.J. & Sharp, A.M. (1995). *Teaching for better thinking: The classroom community of inquiry.* Melbourne: ACER.

Van Rossem, K., Meskens, J., & Van Overmeir, J. (2017). *Leerling of Bekeerling? Radicalisering bespreken in de klas.* Leuven: Acco.

Worley, P. (2021). *Corrupting youth.* Volume 1 and Volume 2. London: Rowman & Littlefield.

2. Read more about Socrates and the Socratic dialogue

Beversluis, J. (2000). *Cross-examining Socrates: A defence of the interlocutors in Plato's early dialogues.* Cambridge: Cambridge University Press.

Boers, E. (2022). *From science to conscience: Socratic dialogue revisited.* Enschede: Gildeprint.

Bolten, H. (2001). Managers develop moral accountability: The impact of Socratic dialogue. *Philosophy of Management* 1 (3): pp. 21–34.

Bolten, H. & Van Rossem, K. (2014). Socratisch beraad. In: Van Dartel, H. & Molewijk, B. (eds.). *In gesprek blijven over goede zorg* (pp. 96–112). Amsterdam: Boom.

Kessels, J., Boers, E., & Mostert, P. (2009). *Free space: Field guide to conversations.* Amsterdam: Boom.

Matthews, G. (2002). *Socratic perplexity and the nature of philosophy.* Oxford: Oxford University Press.

Nelson, L. (1922). The Socratic method. Reprinted in Saran, R. & Neisser, B. (2004). *Enquiring minds.* Trentham: Trentham Books.

Plato (1961). *The collected dialogues of Plato*. Translated by E. Hamilton and H. Cairns. Princeton: Princeton University Press.

Plato (1999). *Collected works*. Translated by X. de Win. Kapellen/ Baarn: Pelckmans Agora.

Reich, R. (1998). Confusion about the Socratic method: Socratic paradoxes and contemporary invocations of Socrates. *Philosophy of Education*, pp. 68–78.

Scott, G. (ed.) (2002). *Does Socrates have a method? Rethinking the elenchus in Plato's dialogues and beyond*. Pennsylvania: Pennsylvania University Press.

Sluiter, I. (2014). *Socrates*. Amsterdam: Amsterdam University Press.

Van Rossem, K. (2014). Meeting Socrates: How to do Socratic consultations. *Philosophical Practice: Journal of the APPA*, 9 (1), pp. 1344–1351.

Van Rossem, K. (2017). Le dialogue socratique en pratique. In: De Moor, M. (ed.), *Socrate à l'Agora: Que peut la parole philosophique* (pp. 64–77). Paris: Vrin.

Van Rossem, K. (2018). How to lead a Socratic dialogue. In: Staude, D. & Ruschmann, E. (eds.), *Understanding the other and oneself* (pp. 67–80). Cambridge: Cambridge Scholars.

3. Stimuli, work formats, and useful exercises

Anthone, R. & Moors, S. (2007). *Van boeken ga je denken: Filosoferen met kinderen bij de hand van jeugdliteratuur*. Leuven: Acco.

Haynes, J. & Murris, K. (2012). *Picturebooks, pedagogy and philosophy*. London: Routledge.

Worley, P. (2011). *The if machine: Philosophical enquiry in the classroom*. London: Bloomsbury.

Worley, P. & Philosophy Foundation (Waltham, Mass.) (2012). *The philosophy shop: Ideas, activities and questions to get people, young and old, thinking philosophically*. Wales: Independent Thinking Press.

4. Useful websites

www.filosofieonderwijs.be. Flemish Network for Contemporary Philosophy Education (VEFO)

www.kinderfilosofie.nl. Centre for P4C Holland

www.sophianetwork.eu/. Sophia: European Foundation for the Advancement of Doing Philosophy with Children

http://my.icpic.org/. ICPIC: International Council of Philosophical Inquiry with Children

www.montclair.edu/cehs/academics/centers-and-institutes/iapc/. Institute for the Advancement of Philosophy for Children

www.philosophisch-politische-akademie.de. The German "mother house" of the Socratic method

www.socraticdialogue.be. The website of Kristof Van Rossem

CHANGEMAKERS
BOOKS

Transform your life, transform our world. Changemakers
Books publishes books for people who seek to become positive,
powerful agents of change. These books inform, inspire,
and provide practical wisdom and skills to empower us to
write the next chapter of humanity's future.
www.changemakers-books.com

The Resilience Series

The Resilience Series is a collaborative effort by the
authors of Changemakers Books in response to the 2020
coronavirus pandemic. Each concise volume offers expert
advice and practical exercises for mastering specific skills
and abilities. Our intention is that by strengthening your
resilience, you can better survive and even thrive in
a time of crisis.
www.resiliencebooks.com

Adapt and Plan for the New Abnormal – in the COVID-19 Coronavirus Pandemic
Gleb Tsipursky

Aging with Vision, Hope and Courage in a Time of Crisis
John C. Robinson

Connecting with Nature in a Time of Crisis
Melanie Choukas-Bradley

Going Within in a Time of Crisis
P. T. Mistlberger

Grow Stronger in a Time of Crisis
Linda Ferguson

Handling Anxiety in a Time of Crisis
George Hoffman

Navigating Loss in a Time of Crisis
Jules De Vitto

The Life-Saving Skill of Story
Michelle Auerbach

Virtual Teams – Holding the Center When You Can't Meet Face-to-Face
Carlos Valdes-Dapena

Virtually Speaking – Communicating at a Distance
Tim Ward and Teresa Erickson

Current Bestsellers from Changemakers Books

Pro Truth
A Practical Plan for Putting Truth Back into Politics
Gleb Tsipursky and Tim Ward
How can we turn back the tide of post-truth politics, fake news, and misinformation that is damaging our democracy? In the lead-up to the 2020 US Presidential Election, Pro Truth provides the answers.

An Antidote to Violence
Evaluating the Evidence
Barry Spivack and Patricia Anne Saunders
It's widely accepted that Transcendental Meditation can create peace for the individual, but can it create peace in society as a whole? And if it can, what could possibly be the mechanism?

Finding Solace at Theodore Roosevelt Island
Melanie Choukas-Bradley
A woman seeks solace on an urban island paradise in Washington D.C. through 2016–17, and the shock of the Trump election.

the bottom
a theopoetic of the streets
Charles Lattimore Howard
An exploration of homelessness fusing theology, jazz-verse and intimate storytelling into a challenging, raw and beautiful tale.

The Soul of Activism
A Spirituality for Social Change
Shmuly Yanklowitz
A unique examination of the power of interfaith spirituality to
fuel the fires of progressive activism.

Future Consciousness
The Path to Purposeful Evolution
Thomas Lombardo
An empowering evolutionary vision of wisdom and the human
mind to guide us in creating a positive future.

Preparing for a World that Doesn't Exist – Yet
Rick Smyre and Neil Richardson
This book is about an emerging Second Enlightenment and
the capacities you will need to achieve success in this new,
fast-evolving world.